A MAN CALLED OTTO

FADE IN:

1   I/E. BUSY BEAVER HARDWARE STORE, 2018 - DAY   1

OUTSIDE - the words "BUSY BEAVER" are spelled out across the front of the hardware store in bold letters.

INSIDE - OTTO (63, irascible) mutters his way through the aisles. He picks out a large screw hook, examines various kinds of rope. Finally settling on one, he measures five feet and pulls out a pocket knife to cut it.

A teenaged HARDWARE CLERK approaches wearing a shirt that reads: *"Need Help? Ask a Beaver."*

                HARDWARE CLERK
Can I help you with that, sir?

                OTTO
       (Turning, incredulous:)
You think I don't know how to cut rope?

                HARDWARE CLERK
No, it's just that we usually do that for you.

                OTTO
I'm not an invalid!

                HARDWARE CLERK
No, I - I didn't think you were.

                OTTO
Are you worried I'm going to cut myself? Bleed all over your floor, then sue you for it?

                HARDWARE CLERK
No.

                OTTO
Well, then -

Otto gestures for the clerk to leave him in peace. A beat; the clerk goes. Otto begins sawing through the rope.

                                      CUT TO:

THE HARDWARE COUNTER - Otto sets the rope and screw hook on the counter. The young clerk begins ringing up his purchase.

                    HARDWARE CLERK
          Did you... find everything you were
          looking for?

Otto grunts, nods. The clerk measures the rope against a
yardstick glued to the counter and adds it to Otto's total.

                    HARDWARE CLERK (CONT'D)
          Good... Okay. That'll be $3.47.

                    OTTO
               (Squints at the register:)
          You charged me for six feet of
          rope.

                    HARDWARE CLERK
          Yes. It's 99 cents a yard.

                    OTTO
          But I didn't get two yards. I got
          five feet.

                    HARDWARE CLERK
          We don't charge by the foot, we
          charge by the yard.

                    OTTO
          99 cents a yard is 33 cents a foot -
          times five, that's $1.65.

                    HARDWARE CLERK
          I know, but I can't put it into the
          computer that way.

                    OTTO
          What the hell kind of computer
          can't do simple math?

                    HARDWARE CLERK
          Yeah... I'm sorry. I think they
          sell rope by the foot over at the
          Home Depot if you want.

                    OTTO
          I don't want to go to the goddamn
          Home Depot! Where's your manager?

                    HARDWARE CLERK
          He's at lunch.

                    OTTO
               (Shaking his head:)
          Lunch.
                    (MORE)

OTTO (CONT'D)
All anyone wants to do anymore is go to lunch. Is anyone else in charge?

HARDWARE CLERK
You want the Assistant Manager?

OTTO
Yes!

HARDWARE CLERK
Hey, Taylor!

TAYLOR (a baby-faced teen) appears at the back of the store.

TAYLOR
What's up?

OTTO
(To the Clerk, squinting:)
She's the Assistant Manager? How old is she?
(To Taylor:)
Shouldn't you be in gym class?

TAYLOR
... Sorry - what?

Another HARDWARE CUSTOMER (male, 40s) who has gotten in line behind Otto digs in his pocket for change.

HARDWARE CUSTOMER
Here, I have some change. Let me cover that extra 33 cents for you -

OTTO
I don't want your 33 cents! This isn't about 33 cents! This is about the fact that I only got five feet of rope and I shouldn't have to pay for six feet unless I get six feet!

TAYLOR
Do you want another foot of rope?

Otto turns to gape at her, astounded.

INT. OTTO'S HOUSE - BEFORE DAWN

IN MONTAGE - Otto goes about his morning routine:

- OTTO'S DARKENED BEDROOM: the moment the clock by Otto's bedside hits 5:30 am, his eyes open - no alarm necessary.

- BATHROOM: Otto stands before the mirror, electric shaver in hand. He regards himself in the mirror a beat, then turns the shaver on and begins shaving.

- BEDROOM: Otto takes a quarter from a dish on his bedside table, tucks it in his shirt pocket, heads downstairs.

- KITCHEN/DINING ROOM: Otto sets two cups on the table next to a bear-shaped honey dispenser. He pours coffee in one cup, sits. Raises his cup, gives a nod and toasts, sips. He finishes his coffee, checks the clock - 5:58 - rises.

3   EXT. OTTO'S HOUSE/NEIGHBORHOOD - MORNING (MONTAGE)   3

- Otto steps OUTSIDE, annoyed to see an ad flyer lying on his front walk. As he picks it up, he becomes aware of an acrid scent. He bends down and sniffs the sidewalk, glowers.

- OTTO'S STREET: Otto checks cars for parking permits and picks up all the flyers tossed in front of homes.

   The homes on this street share exterior walls. Signs have been placed in front of several saying they're "Available for Lease by BIRCHWOOD REALTY - A DYE & MERICA Company."

   JIMMY (20s), a heavyset young man in a sweatsuit, power-walks past Otto swinging tiny hand weights.

                    JIMMY
          Hey Otto!

   Otto barely nods, continues onward.

- Otto goes to the RECYCLING BINS near the row of garages at the end of the street and throws out all the flyers he's collected. He notices people have mixed their glass and paper together despite angry posted signs and uses a reach extender tool to sort items into the right bins.

   A bike leans against one of the bins. Otto rolls it over to a bike rack. A teenager, MALCOLM (17, transgender boy, perceived as a boy by others) runs up toward Otto.

                    MALCOLM
          Hey! What the hell - ? That's mine!

                    OTTO
          It belongs on the bike rack.

                    MALCOLM
          I was only gone half a minute!

                    OTTO
          The next time, I'm locking it in
          the lost and found.

                    MALCOLM
               (Riding away, under his
                breath:)
          Grumpy old bastard...

- As Otto heads up the block, he notices REUBEN (60s, African-American, in a wheelchair), gazing vacantly out the front window of his home as his wife, ANITA, tries to feed him.

Anita glances up. Otto looks away, headed onward toward...

- The GATE that restricts traffic at the far end of the street. A sign posted on the gate reads:

            THIS IS NOT A THRU STREET
          CARS WITH REGISTERED PERMITS ONLY
          NO PARKING FOR BIRCHWOOD ESTATES

On the far side of the gate, across the road, a staircase leads up to Birchwood Estates, a complex of newer condos.

Otto tugs on the gate to make sure it's latched, then notices tire tracks in the grass to one side where someone has driven around the gate. He glares across the street at a sign that reads: "Birchwood Estates - Main offices."

Otto notices ANDY (late 20s, wearing yoga pants) jogging up and down the Birchwood steps. Andy waves as he goes into a series of groin stretches. Otto, turns away, vaguely ill.

- As Otto heads back, he sees BARB (20s, sunglasses, heels) walking her little dog PRINCE. Otto calls out to her.

                    OTTO
          Don't you dare let that little rat
          dog of yours piss on my walkway
          again! I know it was you!

Barb stiffens. She guides Prince quickly past Otto.

                    BARB
          Ignore him, Prince. He's a nasty,
          bitter old man. And he has no idea
          who's doing that.

                    OTTO
          Well, it was one of you -

Otto swings a foot in the dog's general direction.

                              BARB
                    Oh, my God!

          Otto continues walking, calling over his shoulder.

                              OTTO
                    And tell your useless boyfriend to
                    stop stretching his groin in
                    public! He's dressed like a 14-year
                    old Romanian gymnast, for God's
                    sake!

          - Otto takes out his keys, walking to his GARAGE, then stops.
          A MANGY CAT with patchy fur stands in front of the garage
          door. It has half a tail, one ear, and a squint in one eye,
          which it uses to size up Otto like a gunslinger.

          Otto stomps toward The Cat, expecting to scare it off. The
          Cat raises its head, puffs out what fur it has left and
          hisses. Otto pauses, surprised and a little impressed -
          then he hisses back, charging forward and waving his arms.

                              OTTO (CONT'D)
                    Go on! Get out of here!

          The Cat watches Otto charge, gives what looks like a
          disdainful roll of the eyes, then turns and saunters off.

          Otto opens his garage door and goes inside, then drives his
          10-year old Chevy Malibu out, headed to...

    4   EXT. STIMCO STEEL AND ALUMINUM FABRICATION CORP. - DAY   4

          Otto arrives in the parking lot of "STIMCO STEEL."

    5   INT. STIMCO STEEL PRODUCTION FLOOR/MAIN OFFICE - CONTINUOUS 5

          Otto enters and crosses the open production floor.
          METALWORKERS in hardhats weld, bend and shape steel rods and
          metal sheeting into various shapes; others use beam cranes
          and overhead winches to load trucks with beams and rebar.

          Otto climbs a short staircase and goes into the front room of
          the MAIN OFFICE, bewildered to find a group of CO-WORKERS
          huddled inside waiting for him. A tepid cheer goes up among
          the workers as they gather around Otto with anxious smiles.
          Otto notices a cake on a nearby table with his picture on it
          and the words "Congratulations Otto," along with a stack of
          plates, cups, soda and balloons.

          Otto's BOSS (40s) comes forward, clapping and smiling.

                    BOSS
          There he is - the big man himself!

He approaches Otto with open arms, intending to give him an
embrace - but when he sees Otto's sullen demeanor, he quickly
abandons the notion, giving Otto two thumbs up instead.

The applause dies. Otto nods toward the cake.

                    OTTO
          What is this?

                    BOSS
          It's a... well, retirement cake, I
          guess - call it what you like.

                    OTTO
          "Have Fun?" Doing what?

                    BOSS
          With the rest of your life. We
          wanted to, you know...

                    OTTO
          Celebrate?

                    BOSS
          Yes - well, no - give you a nice
          send-off.

                    OTTO
          What's nice about it?

                    BOSS
          Come on, Otto. You're the one who
          decided to leave - and you did get
          a nice severance package.

                    OTTO
          You took me off Operations, you cut
          back my hours, and you made Terry,
          who I trained, my supervisor -
              (Pointing to a colleague:)
          Terry - who can barely figure out
          what year it is without a
          calculator. So yes, I took the
          severance package.

Awkward pause. Terry sulks. Some look shocked, others fight
back laughter. A few look as though they want to applaud.

                    BOSS
          I'm sorry you see it that way. We
          all had to adjust after the merger.
              (MORE)

                    BOSS (CONT'D)
          But you've been quite an asset to
          this company over the years, so -

A couple CO-WORKERS chime in.

                    CO-WORKER 1
          You have. Reliable as hell.

                    CO-WORKER 2
          We're going to miss those schedules
          of yours!

The others laugh. The Boss grabs a cake knife from the desk, starts to offer it to Otto, then reconsiders, handing it to CO-WORKER 1. The Boss grabs a plastic cup, raises a toast.

                    BOSS
          To Otto!

                    CO-WORKERS
          To Otto!

Another cheer. Someone turns on music. CO-WORKER 1 cuts the cake, slicing through the pic of Otto's face on the icing.

                    CO-WORKER 1
          Hey, Otto - you want a piece of
          your face?

Beat. Otto turns to his boss, pointing through a window toward his desk in the adjoining room.

                    OTTO
          How am I supposed to finish work
          today with all this going on?

                    BOSS
          You don't have to work today. Have
          some cake, why don't you?

                    OTTO
          I still have open orders to fill.

                    BOSS
          Don't worry about those. I gave
          them all to Terry. You're done.

Beat. Otto crosses into his office and takes a small photo of a beautiful woman (SONYA) from his desk. The others watch, stunned, as he goes back through the front room and leaves the office without a word.

                              BOSS (CONT'D)
                         (Gesturing to the cake:)
                    Who's hungry?

                              TERRY
                    I'll have a piece of his face.

6   I/E. OTTO'S CHEVY MALIBU/OTTO'S STREET - DAY   6

         The gates are open when Otto drives up. He pulls through and
         jumps out of his car to accost a UPS DRIVER who has just
         dropped a package off.

                              OTTO
                    Hey! If you don't have a permit,
                    you can't use this road!

                              UPS DRIVER
                    I'm not parking. I just dropped off
                    a package.

                              OTTO
                    The sign doesn't say anything about
                    packages, does it? It says no -

         The UPS Driver jumps in the truck, not waiting for more.

                              UPS DRIVER
                    Have a nice day, sir!

         The UPS truck drives off through the open gate.

7   INT. OTTO'S KITCHEN/LIVING ROOM/BEDROOM - DAY/MONTAGE   7

         Otto's phone is ringing when he enters his house. He answers.

                              TELEMARKETER (V.O. - ON PHONE)
                    Oh, hi - sorry, can you hear me?
                    It's Susan. I have great news about
                    your life insurance -

         Otto starts to interrupt, then realizes the call is pre-
         recorded. He hangs up in frustration. After a beat, he picks
         up a handwritten address book, finds the number for the phone
         company and dials. A Phone Rep answers on the other end.

                              OTTO
                    ... Yes, you can help me. I want
                    this phone line disconnected.

         IN QUICK SUCCESSION (LOOSE ENDS MONTAGE):

- Otto flips through his address book, phone pressed to his ear.

> OTTO (CONT'D)
> Yes, I want my electricity shut off... As soon as possible...

- He speaks to the GAS COMPANY:

> OTTO (CONT'D)
> Then why can't you just refund me for six days?... No! If I have to pay for six more days, you're going to keep the goddamn gas on six more days!... Good - we're done!

OTTO HANGS UP, closes his address book...

- PULLS OUT THE TRASH...

- VACUUMS the LIVING ROOM...

- UP IN HIS BEDROOM, Otto puts on his best suit and tie, transfers the quarter from his work shirt into the breast pocket of his jacket.

END MONTAGE.

8   INT. OTTO'S LIVING ROOM - DAY   8

Otto moves the coffee table, puts newspaper down on the floor and sets a chair down on top. Otto's drill is on the side table, along with the rope and screw hook he purchased.

Otto climbs onto the chair and knocks on the ceiling to find the joist. He drills a hole in the ceiling, twists the screw hook into it, then makes a noose and ties it on.

As he starts to slip the noose over his head, he notices a framed picture of Sonya on the side table. Otto climbs down and turns the picture around so Sonya isn't watching him.

He gets back onto the chair, puts the noose around his neck. As he starts to lean forward, he hears a loud scraping sound.

Otto looks out through the blinds, stunned to see that someone with a trailer hitched to their car has backed their trailer up onto the sidewalk across the street.

> OTTO
> What the - ?! Oh, for - !

He pulls his head out of the noose and hurries to the door.

9   EXT. OTTO'S HOUSE - DAY   9

Otto rushes outside and crosses the street, directing his anger at an extremely pregnant woman (MARISOL, 30, Latina) who was apparently trying to direct the parking job.

> OTTO
> What the hell are you doing?

> MARISOL
> (Mexican accent:)
> Yes, that's what I was saying –
> (Turning to the car:)
> *¿Que diablos estàs haciendo?*

She sounds angrier than Otto, which throws him.

> OTTO
> Look, you can't just drive in here –

> MARISOL
> *I'm* not driving, am I?

Flustered, Otto turns to TOMMY (30s, Latino) the tall, oddly cheerful guy who's just climbed out of the car.

> OTTO
> You aren't allowed to bring a car in here without a permit.

> TOMMY
> (Mexican accent:)
> We have one! Here –

Tommy digs in his pocket and produces the permit that is supposed to hang on his rearview mirror.

> OTTO
> Why the hell is it in your pocket?

> TOMMY
> I'm the driver.

> MARISOL
> (Pointing to a house:)
> We're renting here. 206.

> OTTO
> That doesn't mean you can back the trailer up to your front door.

> TOMMY
> I wasn't. I was parallel parking.

                    OTTO
          Parallel to *what??*

                    TOMMY
          Yeah - it didn't go so well. No
          real harm done at least.

Otto points to the rear end of the trailer, which is pushing against the low bushes in front of the house they're renting.

                    OTTO
          You're in the flowerbed!

                    TOMMY
          That's not really a flowerbed, is
          it?

                    OTTO
          Not anymore, it isn't!

Tommy looks to Marisol. She glares at him. Tommy realizes he's outnumbered, heads back to the car.

                    TOMMY
          Okay... I'll give it another try.

Otto and Marisol watch as Tommy struggles to climb into the tiny car, both shaking their heads and sighing.

          OTTO   MARISOL
My God.   *Dios mío.*

Tommy closes his door and starts the engine. The car lurches into the street, then backs up, heading over the curb once again, straight toward the front of the house.

                    OTTO (CONT'D)
          STOP!

Otto storms forward and yanks open the car door.

                    TOMMY
          My bad! I thought I was home free -

                    OTTO
          Get out of the car!

Tommy gets out, abashed. Otto pushes him aside and climbs in.

                    OTTO (CONT'D)
          How you can have made it this far
          in life without knowing how to back
          up a trailer?
                         (MORE)

                    OTTO (CONT'D)
          My God, a dog with one front paw
          and cataracts could have done
          better than that.

Otto shuts the door, shaking his head when he sees the
digital instrument panel.

                    OTTO (CONT'D)
          Automatic, of course.
              (Rolling down the window:)
          Give me the keys.

                    TOMMY
          They're in the cupholder. But it's
          a push button start.

                    OTTO
          I know!

Otto looks around for the push button start.

                    TOMMY
          It's still running. The engine
          shuts off when you stop -

                    OTTO
          I know!

Otto puts the car in reverse. An electronic bell sounds.

                    OTTO (CONT'D)
          What the - ?

                    TOMMY
              (Pointing to the dash:)
          That's the radar. It goes off in
          reverse because the trailer's so
          close to the back of the -

Otto rolls the window up, cutting off further discussion. He
pulls forward and looks over his shoulder - finally noticing
the two children, LUNA (7) and ABBIE (5), who are sitting in
the back seat.

                    LUNA
          Hello.

                    OTTO
          Hello.

The bell sounds again as Otto begins backing the trailer into
the parking spot.

                    LUNA
               What's your name?

                    OTTO
               Otto.

Abbie's never heard this name before and finds it funny.

                    ABBIE
               Oddo?

                    OTTO
               Otto. O-t-t-o.

                    ABBIE
               I'm Abbie, O-t-t-o.

                    LUNA
               And I'm Luna.

                    OTTO
               Nice to meet you.

He stops the car in front of his house, throws it in park and gets out, marching back toward Tommy to hand him the keys.

                    OTTO (CONT'D)
               You should turn that radar crap
               off. Anyone who thinks they need
               radar to back up a car shouldn't be
               doing it in the first place.

                    TOMMY
               Thanks for the help.

                    OTTO
               They shouldn't even be allowed to
               use the radio.

Otto catches Marisol's eye. She looks like she's trying not to laugh. Otto walks back toward his house, calling:

                    OTTO (CONT'D)
               The permit goes on your rearview
               mirror, not in your damn pocket.

10   INT. OTTO'S HOUSE - DAY   10

Otto enters and closes the door behind him, muttering:

                    OTTO
               Idiot...

Otto sinks onto a bench in the hall, exhausted. He glances up at the sea of women's coats that hang on wall pegs, light from the windows drifting across the space as time passes -

And then the lights click off.

Otto glances around. He rises, goes into the living room, tries the light switch. Nothing. His power has been shut off.

He opens the window blinds, then realizes the noose is visible from outside and shuts them enough to block the view.

Otto turns to look at the noose. Beat. He straightens his suit, climbs onto the chair, then stops, noticing something.

Otto climbs back down, fixes the pillows on the couch. He goes to the bookcase and straightens the books, pausing to glance at a few of the titles, drifting back in his memory...

FLASH BACK TO:

The light in the room changes, the blinds fully open. Otto is still in his 60s, but the scene he remembers takes place in 1980, decades earlier, and the room reflects it.

WOMAN'S VOICE (O.S.)
How much more shelf space is left?

Otto turns, watching as SONYA (25) enters carrying a box.

OTTO
Three shelves. How many boxes of
books do you have left?

Sonya walks past Otto and sets the box of books on the side table. As the camera follows Sonya, we see YOUNG OTTO (25) reflected in a darkened television screen across the room.

SONYA
Seven or eight.

Young Otto picks the box up from the side table.

YOUNG OTTO
Then I'll build you another
bookcase.

Pan back to Otto (63) still lost in memory. As he crosses the room, the light fades, and when he gets to the side table, Sonya, Young Otto and the book box are all gone.

Otto gazes at his older reflection in the television, the noose still hanging from the ceiling behind him.

                                        END FLASHBACK.

Otto climbs back on the chair and tightens the noose. The doorbell rings. Otto pauses, exasperated. Another knock.

                    OTTO
          Damnit! Damnit! Damnit!

Otto climbs down and goes to the front door...

11   I/E. OTTO'S HALLWAY, FRONT DOOR - CONTINUOUS   11

... Throwing it open. Marisol and Tommy are outside. Marisol holds a Tupperware container.

NOTE: Marisol pronounces Otto's name with a long 'O' ("Oh-to") instead of the broad Midwestern pronunciation Otto uses ("Ah-to").

                    MARISOL
          Hello. Otto, yes? The girls said –

                    OTTO
          "AH-to."

                    MARISOL
              (Bewildered:)
          That's what I said. What did I say?

                    OTTO
          Doesn't matter what you said. It's
          O-t-t-o.

                    MARISOL
          So it's the same frontwards as
          backwards: *"Oh-toh."*

                    OTTO
          "AH-to!"

                    TOMMY
          You don't hear that name too often
          these days, do you?

                    OTTO
          <u>I</u> do.

                    MARISOL
          Are we interrupting? We can always –

                    OTTO
          What? What do you want?

                    MARISOL
               (Holds up the container:)
          I brought you some food.

                    OTTO
          ... Why?

                    MARISOL
          Because you looked hungry.

                    TOMMY
          That's why we go so well together.
          She likes to cook and I like to...

Tommy gestures to his large frame. Otto doesn't react. Tommy grows awkward, not knowing whether to smile or look away.

                    TOMMY (CONT'D)
          ... eat ...

                    MARISOL
          Anyway, we wanted to introduce
          ourselves properly now that we're
          going to be neighbors.

She offers him the Tupperware container. Otto nods, takes it.

                    OTTO
          Okay. Bye.

He starts to close the door. Marisol places her foot onto the threshold, speaking in the tone of a mother teaching manners.

                    MARISOL
          <u>My name is Marisol</u>.

Otto stares at the foot in disbelief, then raises his head to look Marisol in the eye.

                    TOMMY
          I'm Tommy.

Otto and Marisol, eyes locked, pay no mind to Tommy.

                    MARISOL
          Are you always this unfriendly?

                    OTTO
          I am not unfriendly!

                    MARISOL
          No? I'd say you are a little
          unfriendly.

                    OTTO
          I am not!

                    MARISOL
          No, you are right. Your every word
          is like a warm cuddle, really.

Beat. Otto takes his hand off the door handle. He glances
down at the Tupperware container, lifts a corner of the lid.

                    OTTO
          Chicken and rice?

                    MARISOL
          Pollo mole - it's a Mexican dish. I
          was born in el Salvador, that's
          where my father was from, but my
          mother was Mexican - she went down
          to El Salvador to run an
          agriculture program. So that's how
          they met, and that's where I was
          born. But I grew up in Mexico.

Otto nods, gestures to Tommy with the container.

                    OTTO
          What about you?

                    TOMMY
          I'm an I.T. consultant.

Otto and Marisol sigh.

                    MARISOL
              (To Tommy:)
          Dile de dónde eres.

                    TOMMY
          Oh. Anaheim.

                    OTTO
          Anaheim?

                    TOMMY
              (Shrugs.)
          ... El Paso.

Otto nods, then reaches for the door handle.

                    OTTO
          Well, I have things I need to do -

                    TOMMY
          You wouldn't have an Alvin wrench I
          could borrow, would you?

                    OTTO
              (Takes this in, squints:)
          You mean an Allen wrench.

                    TOMMY
          No, it's Alvin.

                    OTTO AND MARISOL
          Allen!

                    MARISOL
              (To Otto:)
          I told him and he was like -
              (Mocking Tommy's accent:)
          "Umm, no, it's an Alvin Wrench."

                    TOMMY
          Well, everyone else I know calls it
          an Alvin Wrench.

                    MARISOL
          Then everyone else is wrong.

                    OTTO
          Good God...

Otto steps outside and heads down toward his garage as they
continue bickering.

                    TOMMY
          You want to Google it?

                    MARISOL
          Sure. Google it! Wikipedia it!

                    TOMMY
          Fine - give me your phone!

                    MARISOL
          ¡Usa tu teléfono!

                    TOMMY
          ¡A ver, no seas así!

AT THE GARAGE - Otto retrieves his Allen wrench set from his
workbench and returns to Tommy outside.

                    OTTO
          Do you know what size you need?

                    TOMMY
          Just the usual size.

Otto winces. He hands Tommy the wrench set and closes the
garage door.

                    OTTO
          Take the set.

                    TOMMY
          Wow. Thanks.

                    MARISOL
          Yes, thank you, Otto. Come along,
          Tommy - Otto has things to do.

Otto watches them go back to their house, then notices the
Mangy Cat has shown up and is now staring at him.

                    OTTO
          What do you want? Huh?

They gaze at each other a beat, then Otto heads back to his
house.

12   I/E. OTTO'S HOUSE - DAY   12

    Otto enters the DINING ROOM/KITCHEN and sits at the table. He
    notices the Tupperware container in his hands. Pause.

    He opens the lid, sniffs it, then gets a fork and sits down
    to eat, staring at the noose in the living room as he chews.

    There is food left over when Otto finishes. He goes to the
    trash can, realizes he hasn't replaced the bag. Beat. He gets
    a colorful bowl out of the cupboard, scoops the leftovers
    into it and takes it OUTSIDE for the Mangy Cat to finish.

    Otto sets the bowl on the stoop and turns to go - then
    reconsiders, moving the bowl further from the front door
    before going back inside.

    Otto returns to the LIVING ROOM, climbs up on the chair.

    He tightens the noose around his neck, braces himself...

    ... Then kicks the stool out from under him.

    As Otto struggles, memories of Sonya flash through his mind
    ('LIFE FLASHES PAST' MONTAGE) -

- OTTO'S POV: Sonya drops a book on a TRAIN PLATFORM. It is 1973; she's just 18 years old...

- She sits across from him in the DINING ROOM of their new home (1980), raising a coffee cup in a toast and smiling...

- She lies in BED, slips her finger into Otto's open palm...

PRE-LAP: A disconnected voice, that of OTTO'S FATHER...

> OTTO'S FATHER (O.S.)
> Isn't she beautiful, son?

- A BOYHOOD MEMORY, 1965 (POV CONTINUES) - Otto remembers gazing up at his Father as he opens the hood of a 1950s CHEVY IMPALA and looks at the engine approvingly.

> OTTO'S FATHER (CONT'D)
> Carburetor, spark plugs, pistons -
> it all works together, nothing's
> wasted. That's a Chevy engine for
> you. Dependable. Not enough you can
> depend on in this world...

The scene fades from view as (OUT OF POV)...

BACK IN OTTO'S LIVING ROOM (INTERCUT) - Otto's struggling slows. He drifts back into memory one last time...

- OTTO'S POV: Sonya's face appears. It is 1983; she is 29. She smiles, but there are tears in her eyes.

> SONYA
> That's enough now, darling...

As she reaches out to touch Otto's cheek, Otto's vision BLURS TO WHITE...

OUT OF POV - the world around Otto begins spinning, the LIVING ROOM fading from view.

PULL BACK as debris seems to fly through the air all around Otto. He hears his father's voice one last time...

> OTTO'S FATHER (V.O.)
> If you're going to make something,
> Otto, learn how to make it right...

END FLASHBACK MONTAGE.

BACK IN OTTO'S LIVING ROOM - CRACK! The dried wood of the ceiling joist gives way and the screw hook pulls free. Otto falls into the present, crashing to the floor, coughing.

He yanks the noose off and throws it down in disgust. He
starts to get up, then hesitates, wincing as he grips his
left arm. The pain gradually fades. Otto notices a coupon in
the newspaper on the floor for flowers - two for eight
dollars.

13   EXT. CEMETERY - SUNSET/DUSK   13

Otto walks across an expanse of grass carrying a lawn chair,
a thermos, and some potted flowers. He unfolds the lawn
chair, puts the thermos beside it.

> OTTO
> I found the flowers you like. Pink.

Otto sets the flowers in front of the grave marker of SONYA
ANDERSON. He clears away old flowers, leaves and twigs.

> OTTO (CONT'D)
> Sorry I didn't come earlier. I got
> distracted by the new neighbors.
> The husband doesn't know his ass
> from an Allen wrench.
>   (He sits. Scornfully:)
> They're *renters,* of course. No
> commitment to anything.

Otto reacts as though he's heard Sonya disagree with him.

> OTTO (CONT'D)
> I know - maybe they can't afford to
> buy yet, but where will they be
> when those real estate bastards
> decide to tear that house down and
> put up more shit condos? Because it
> will happen, I promise you. They're
> already driving on the grass.
>   (He shakes his head.)
> *"Dye & Merica"* - what idiot thought
> that was a good name for a real
> estate company? Sounds like 'dying
> America'... It is, I suppose. Can't
> even buy a decent screw hook
> anymore.
>   (Long pause.)
> Nothing works when you're not home.

13A   EXT. OTTO'S HOUSE - NIGHT   13A

Darkness. A light snow falls.

14   INT. OTTO'S BEDROOM - EARLY MORNING   14

The next morning. Otto's eyes are still shut. He shifts as he dreams, stretching a hand toward the other side of the bed.

IN HIS DREAMS, Sonya lies beside him in bed. She reaches over and slips her index finger into his palm...

Otto's eyes open. His hand is empty. He glances at the clock, surprised that it's only 5:12. Otto lies back down, then gazes at the window curtains beside his bed, remembering...

                                        MATCH CUT TO:

15   EXT. MILITARY ENTRANCE STATION, 1973 (MEMORY) - DAY   15

Curtains open as a DOCTOR enters an examination area. Otto (still 63) sits on an exam table. Other RECRUITS in their underwear stand in line outside, waiting for their turns.

As the DOCTOR looks at a chart, we see Otto's reflection behind the Doctor in a mirror - as *Young Otto (18)*. The Doctor looks up with a kind smile. The camera turns back to reveal Young Otto sitting on the exam table.

NOTE: In this and other memory sequences, I have indicated when Young Otto appears and which lines of dialogue he speaks. Marc, though, will frequently shoot alternate versions of these sequences in which Otto himself performs the same dialogue in order to have more flexibility in the editing room.

                    ARMY DOCTOR
          ... I suspect you have Hypertrophic
          Cardiomyopathy, which is a genetic
          enlargement of -

                    YOUNG OTTO
          I know. My father had it.

                    ARMY DOCTOR
               (A sympathetic nod.)
          Well, you'll likely be around a
          good long time - but I'm afraid
          your military prospects end here.

16   INT. OTTO'S BEDROOM (2018) - MORNING/INTERCUT   16

CLOSE ON OTTO, back in his bedroom, remembering...

| 17 | EXT. TRAIN TERMINAL, 1973 (MEMORY) - DAY | 17 |

Otto walks through a sleek modern train station. He crosses to a ticket counter, the surface of which is reflective.

As Otto pulls out his wallet to buy a ticket, TILT DOWN to the surface of the counter, revealing *Young Otto's* reflection, then TILT BACK UP - Young Otto now stands at the counter.

Young Otto buys his ticket, then heads down a GATE RAMP that leads to the train platform, lowering his head in embarrassment as he passes young men in uniform.

| 18 | EXT. TRAIN PLATFORM, 1973 (MEMORY) - DAY | 18 |

Young Otto arrives on the Eastbound platform, which is lined with posters of the era; the style of the other PASSENGERS ranges from long hair and tie-dye to crewcuts and business suits.

Young Otto steps up to the track. Sonya appears on the Westbound platform across from him. Young Otto is spellbound.

As Sonya walks along the platform, Otto notices her drop one of the books she carries. He calls to her, but she doesn't hear him because her train is pulling into the station.

Young Otto rushes back into the terminal, up the GATE RAMP and down a set of stairs, appearing a moment later on the Westbound platform. He picks up the book, sees Sonya boarding at the other end of the platform. He starts toward her, then realizes that the train is departing and jumps into the nearest car before the doors close.

| 19 | INT. TRAIN, 1973 (MEMORY) - CONTINUOUS | 19 |

As Young Otto hurries through cars trying to find Sonya, we catch glimpses of *Otto (60s)* reflected in the train windows.

As he hurries through another car, he catches sight of someone out of the corner of his eye. He looks back - and stops his tracks, speechless. Sonya looks up at him. She smiles, not hiding her interest, then sees the book.

                    SONYA
           Is that mine?

                    YOUNG OTTO
          ... What?
               (Glances down, nods, gives
                her the book.)
          Yes.

                    SONYA
          Oh, thank you so much! I'm already
          halfway through - I would hate not
          knowing how it ends.

Young Otto nods. Not knowing what to say, he starts to leave.

                    SONYA (CONT'D)
               (She moves her purse from
                the seat opposite her.)
          Here - why don't you join me?

Young Otto sits, tries not to look as awkward as he feels.

                    SONYA (CONT'D)
          I'm Sonya.

                    YOUNG OTTO
          Otto. It was my father's name.

                    SONYA
          I'm on my way to visit my father
          right now - I go every Thursday. Do
          you take this train a lot?

                    YOUNG OTTO
          No, I had to come into town for my
          army physical.

                    SONYA
               (Eyes wide with sympathy:)
          Oh, God... That must be hard, not
          knowing what you're going to face
          over there. When are you leaving?

                    YOUNG OTTO
          ... Not for a while.

The TRAIN CONDUCTOR comes up alongside their seats.

                    TRAIN CONDUCTOR
          Tickets, please.

Sonya and Young Otto hand him their tickets. The Train
Conductor glances at Young Otto's ticket, hands it back.

                    TRAIN CONDUCTOR (CONT'D)
          I'm afraid you're on the wrong
          train. This is an Eastbound ticket.

                    YOUNG OTTO
               (Fumbles for his wallet.)
          Oh - I must have... I'm getting off
          at the next station. How much - ?

                    TRAIN CONDUCTOR
          $1.75.

Young Otto pulls out his last dollar, searches for change, comes up short. Sonya finds some coins in her purse.

                    SONYA
          Here - I have some change.

                    YOUNG OTTO
          Thank you.

He pays the conductor, then holds a quarter out to Sonya.

                    YOUNG OTTO (CONT'D)
          A quarter to spare.
               (Showing the edge:)
          1964. Pure silver.

                    SONYA
          Keep it then. It's lucky.

She smiles. Otto nods, tucks the coin in his shirt pocket.

                    YOUNG OTTO
          I will pay you back.

                    SONYA
          Don't worry about that for now.

Sonya gestures to the book Otto rescued.

                    SONYA (CONT'D)
          "The Master and Margarita" - have
          you read it?

                    YOUNG OTTO
          No, I... No.

                    SONYA
          I love books. I'm studying to be an
          English teacher. I've always wanted
          to work with kids...

Young Otto drinks Sonya in as she talks, completely smitten. Her words flow by as time passes. He nods along and smiles without fully understanding what she's talking about...

SONYA (CONT'D)
... You know, there's a scene in the book with a draft-dodging cat... for a class on magical realism and fantasy... but I loved "One Hundred Years of Solitude"... Isn't this your stop?

Beat. Young Otto blinks, glances toward the window, the camera following his gaze. The train has stopped. As the camera pans back, we hear *Otto (60s)* answer Sonya's question.

OTTO (O.C.)
Oh, yes...

20 INT. OTTO'S BEDROOM (2018) - MORNING 20

Otto (60s), lies in bed, gazing at his window, remembering.

OTTO
... Yes, it is.

Light has begun creeping in at the window. Otto notices the clock still reads 5:12. He tries to turn on the light. Nothing. Otto gets his watch from the bedside table, looks at it, curses - his alarm clock stopped when the power went out.

He bounds out of bed and pulls a shirt out of his closet, then grabs Sonya's quarter from the dish by his bedside.

21 EXT. OTTO'S HOUSE - DAY 21

Otto hurries outside carrying the empty Tupperware container. It has snowed; a light dusting. He crosses the street and sets Marisol's container on her stoop along with a note: "Thank you. The food was interesting."

LATER, as Otto shovels the snow off his walkway, he notices that the cat bowl he left out the night before is empty.

22 EXT. OTTO'S STREET - DAY 22

Otto makes his rounds. Jimmy power-walks by in a sweatsuit.

JIMMY
Hey Otto! A little late for your morning rounds, isn't it?

                    OTTO
          No.

                    JIMMY
          Aren't you supposed to be at work?

                    OTTO
          No!

                    JIMMY
          Do you want to come over for lunch
          then?

                    OTTO
               (Contemptuous:)
          Lunch!

Otto hears a car engine and turns. A car with the Dye &
Merica logo pulls out of a parking space. As it reaches the
corner, the car turns and bumps up over the curb, intending
to drive around the gate. Otto hurries toward the car, waving
his arms.

                    OTTO (CONT'D)
          Hey! HEY!

                    JIMMY
          See you, Otto!

The car stops. A DYE & MERICA REAL ESTATE AGENT (40s) gets
out.

                    OTTO
          This is a private road! Those gates
          are there to keep down on traffic -
          not for idiots like you to drive
          around them and tear up the grass.

The Agent waves a placating hand. He goes to open the gate.

                    DYE & MERICA AGENT
          Okay - fair enough. You got me.
          I'll have our grounds people come
          over and fix that grass for you.
               (He climbs in his car.)
          You have a good one now, okay?

He shuts his door and drives away, leaving the gate open.

| 23 | EXT. OTTO'S HOUSE - DAY | 23 |

As Otto heads back home, he hears frantic barking. Barb stands out in front of Otto's house, her dog Prince straining at his leash. Otto watches in astonishment as Barb picks up a stone and throws it towards the front of his house.

                BARB
Get out here, you little bitch!

Otto hurries forward, stepping up close behind Barb as she picks up another stone and cocks her arm to throw it.

                OTTO
If you throw one more stone, I swear to God I will drop-kick that dog of yours over the roof.

                BARB
    (Wheels around, glaring:)
I'm not throwing it at your house! That rotten cat scratched Prince! I'm gonna kill that piece of shit!

Otto sees the Mangy Cat cowering behind the low front wall of his porch. The Cat licks a paw, rubs it over a bloodied ear.

                OTTO
No, you won't.

                BARB
What do you care? That thing's feral. It's probably full of all sorts of disgusting diseases.

                OTTO
So are you, most likely, but we don't throw stones at you.

Barb flinches in shock. She sees Andy headed toward them, doing a squat lunge with each step he takes.

                BARB
Andy! Did you hear what he said??

Otto heads for his front door. The Cat stares at him.

                OTTO
Get out of here while you can.
    (Swinging a lazy kick in
     the cat's direction:)
Go on. I'm not your friend.

The Cat is unimpressed, but takes Otto's advice and goes.

| 24 | INT. OTTO'S FRONT DOOR/LIVING ROOM - DAY | 24 |

Otto flicks the front light switch as he enters. Nothing.

He returns to his living room and looks up at the hole in the ceiling where the screw hook pulled out of the joist.

A SHORT TIME LATER - Otto stands on a chair with a roll of duct tape, using it to patch the hole in the ceiling.

There is a knock at the door. Otto sighs, climbs down and crosses to open it. Marisol and Tommy stand outside.

> OTTO
> What now?

> TOMMY
> I brought back your wrenches. I found one that came with the furniture.

> OTTO
> (Taking the wrenches:)
> Congratulations.

> MARISOL
> And I made you *salpors de arroz.*

Marisol holds out another container. Otto squints inside.

> OTTO
> Cookies?

> MARISOL
> *Salvadoran* cookies. They were my father's favorite.

> TOMMY
> You're gonna love them.

> MARISOL
> Of course. I made them.

Otto nods, takes the cookies, starts backing into the house.

> TOMMY
> Also, I was wondering...

Tommy looks to Marisol. She nudges him (*"Go on!"*).

> TOMMY (CONT'D)
> ... If you have a ladder I could borrow. Our window is jammed.

                    OTTO
               (Mystified:)
          Your window is... what??

                    TOMMY
               (Pointing:)
          It's jammed. That one up there. It
          won't open.

                    OTTO
          So you want to try to open it from
          the outside?

                    TOMMY
          Right.

Otto struggles mightily to keep from further comment.

                    OTTO
          Come on, then.

As he leads them DOWN THE STREET, Otto notices Abbie and Luna rolling a ball of snow to start making a snowman; he almost smiles. Abbie waves.

                    ABBIE
          Hola, "O-t-t-o!"

Otto winces a little, but waves back.

                    MARISOL
          Use your English, Abbie.
               (To Otto, explaining:)
          It's the first time they've seen
          snow.

As they round the corner on the way to Otto's garage, they come upon Anita, who is just closing her own garage door.

                    ANITA
          Oh - Otto, good. I hate to bother
          you, but our heat doesn't seem to
          be working. Could you take a look?

                    OTTO
          Try bleeding the radiators.

                    ANITA
          How exactly would I do that?

                    OTTO
          By bleeding the radiators.

Otto opens his own garage door and disappears inside.

                    MARISOL
          Otto! Stop being rude!

                    OTTO (O.S.)
          I'm not being rude!

                    ANITA
          It can be hard to tell the
          difference with Otto sometimes.

                    MARISOL
          We just moved into 206, across from
          Otto. I'm Marisol. This is Tommy.

Anita gives a warm smile, instantly chatty.

                    ANITA
          Welcome to the neighborhood, dear.
          I'm Anita. My husband Reuben used
          to take care of our heat, but he's
          not been well. We always knew the
          day would come when he couldn't
          help around the house any longer.

Otto comes out of his garage carrying the ladder.

                    OTTO
          Maybe Reuben should have thought of
          that when he organized his coup.

                    ANITA
          Oh, please. That was years ago -
               (To Marisol:)
          Otto used to be the head of our
          Homeowner's Association, but when
          the board voted Reuben in, Otto
          quit.

                    OTTO
          It was a coup!

                    MARISOL
          Come on, Otto. Can't you just go
          breathe Anita's radiators for her?

                    OTTO
          You don't *breathe* radiators, for
          God's sake! You bleed them!

Tommy has moved away from the others, noticing a portable
metal ramp just inside the garage. He starts to lift it.

                    TOMMY
          Look at this ramp, Marisol. This is
          what we needed for the trailer.

                    ANITA
          Oh, that was for Sonya -

                    OTTO
               (Furious:)
          What are you doing? Leave my things
          alone! Put that down, take the
          goddamn ladder and get out of here!

                    ANITA
          I'm sorry, Otto. I didn't mean to -

                    OTTO
          GO! All of you!

As they leave, Otto notices Abbie and Luna have been watching
at a distance. They look away, turning back to building their
snowman.

Otto fumbles in frustration and goes close his garage door,
then notices a mangy tail poking out from under his car's
bumper.

                    OTTO (CONT'D)
          Get out from under there!

He swings his foot under the bumper. The Cat yowls and swings
a paw, getting its long claws snagged in Otto's pant leg.

                    OTTO (CONT'D)
          Ow! Let go of me, you little -

Otto pulls his leg back, dragging the Cat out from under the
car. Otto sees that the Cat's claws are stuck in his pants.

                    OTTO (CONT'D)
          Okay, okay - calm down! I'll get
          your claws free, just hold still!
               (Slowly reaching down:)
          If you bite me, I swear to God,
          I'll bite you back.

Otto carefully pulls the Cat's claws free. The Cat scrambles
backward. It turns away from Otto in an attempt at retaining
some dignity, licks its paw, then walks haughtily away.

25   I/E. ANITA AND REUBEN'S HOUSE, FRONT DOOR - DAY   25

Otto walks onto the stoop of Anita and Reuben's house and
knocks. Anita opens the door.

>   ANITA
>   I really am sorry, Otto. I didn't
>   mean to upset you.

Otto grunts, waves a dismissive hand.

>   OTTO
>   I loaned my hose to you in August.
>   Give it back and I'll bleed your
>   radiators for you.

26   INT. ANITA AND REUBEN'S HOUSE, FRONT ENTRY/LIVING ROOM - DAY   26

Anita leads Otto into the living room.

>   ANITA
>   Those new neighbors of yours, they
>   seem lovely, don't they?

Otto grunts.

>   ANITA (CONT'D)
>   I'm afraid you may have more new
>   neighbors soon enough. The realty
>   people, they're telling us Reuben
>   and I have to move out.

>   OTTO
>   That's a load of crap. They don't
>   own this house. You do.

Anita nods, grows emotional. Her hand trembles as she speaks.

>   ANITA
>   That's what I said, but they've
>   been talking to our boy Chris. Now
>   he's saying I can't take care of
>   Reuben anymore, that he needs to go
>   into a special care place and I
>   have to go into a retirement home.

>   OTTO
>   Oh, what does Chris know about it?
>   Chris is an idiot, always has been.
>   They can't make you do anything.

Otto follows Anita into the living room. Reuben sits in his wheelchair by the window. Otto sees his condition up close for the first time - unable to speak and barely able to move.

                    OTTO (CONT'D)
          Does he even know we're here?

                    ANITA
          Of course. Don't let him fool you -
          he's still in there.
               (She turns to go.)
          I'll go look for the hose.

A SHORT TIME LATER: Otto kneels beside the front radiator, talking conspiratorially to Reuben as he bleeds out air.

                    OTTO
          This neighborhood is falling apart
          nowadays. They don't even have a
          Homeowner's Association anymore.
          There's no one to keep things
          running. Not like we did.

He catches a few drops of water in his handkerchief, closes the bleeder valve and rises, turning toward Reuben.

                    OTTO (CONT'D)
          Just to be clear - I still haven't
          forgiven you. I just didn't realize
          you were going to fall to shit so
          quickly. And now they're tearing
          apart everything we worked so hard
          to build. We haven't even left yet
          and they're trying to erase us.

Otto crouches beside Reuben's chair, lowers his voice.

                    OTTO (CONT'D)
          Well, I'm not staying around to see
          that happen. I'm leaving. For good -

Voices approach outside. Anita enters the front door, hose in hand, Jimmy behind her. She hands Otto the hose.

                    ANITA
          Thank you, Otto. I'm sorry it took
          me so long to get this back to you.
          Would you like to stay for lunch?

Otto snorts dismissively.

                    JIMMY
          Anita made a pork tenderloin.

                    OTTO
          No. I have things I need to do.

Otto starts to go, then realizes Reuben has a firm grip on
the hose. Reuben's eyes are fixed on his.

                    ANITA
          Reuben - what are you doing, hon?

                    OTTO
          Let go. Let... go!

Otto pulls the hose from Reuben's grasp. Beat. He walks
stiffly out of the room without looking back.

27   INT. OTTO'S BEDROOM - DAY   27

Otto puts on a suit, fixes his hair. As he crosses to get the
quarter from his bedside table, we see that the hose lies on
the bed. Otto tucks the quarter into his front shirt pocket.

28   EXT. OTTO'S STREET/OTTO'S GARAGE - DAY   28

Otto walks down to his garage carrying the hose and the roll
of duct tape. In the background, Tommy climbs up the ladder
to fix his window.

29   INT. OTTO'S GARAGE/CHEVY MALIBU - CONTINUOUS   29

Otto opens his garage and goes inside, shutting the door
behind him, then opening his car door for light. He duct
tapes the hose into his exhaust pipe, runs the other end in
the back window of the car.

Otto is about to climb in when he sees the container of
cookies on his work bench. He gets a cookie from the
container, then gets into the car and starts the engine.

Otto turns on the radio, searches stations, lands on a
country ballad (*"Til You're Home"*). He listens to the song a
moment while he finishes his cookie, then turns the radio
off, leaning back in his seat as exhaust fills the car...

                              MATCH CUT/FLASH BACK TO:

30   EXT. TRAIN PLATFORM, 1973 - DAY   30

Otto (60s) sits on a train bench, watching people come and
go. It's a foggy morning, dreamlike, hard to recognize faces.

A train pulls in. Otto catches sight of a woman who looks like Sonya boarding at the other end of the platform. He rises, hurries toward her, then tries to board. Too late.

Young Otto's reflection appears in the train windows as the doors close. Young Otto watches as the train leaves the station – then Sonya appears out of the fog, smiling.

> SONYA
> Looks like we'll both have to take the next one.

Young Otto nods, overcome with shyness.

> SONYA (CONT'D)
> Did you have to go back to the military center?

> YOUNG OTTO
> What? Oh. Yes, I...
> (He gathers his courage.)
> No. I wanted to pay you back for the train ticket.

> SONYA
> Wouldn't it be nicer to invite me to dinner?

> YOUNG OTTO
> ... Dinner? Sure, of course... I don't really know how to cook much.

Sonya smiles, finding Otto's innocence incredibly sweet.

> SONYA
> I meant in a restaurant.

Otto smiles, relieved.

31   I/E. RESTAURANT, 1973 - NIGHT   31

A dimly-lit street. Fog. Young Otto paces outside a restaurant, holding flowers, checking his watch. A taxi pulls up; Sonya gets out, beaming.

> SONYA
> Hello!

> YOUNG OTTO
> Hi. Shall we - ?

> SONYA
> Yes, let's go in.

                    YOUNG OTTO
          You're 15 minutes late.

                    SONYA
               (Completely unconcerned:)
          Am I?

32   INT. RESTAURANT, 1973 - NIGHT   32

The couple eats in awkward silence. Sonya has an entrée, Otto
has soup. Young Otto starts to say something. Sonya smiles
expectantly. He changes his mind, has more soup. Finally:

                    SONYA
          So what kinds of things interest
          you?

                    YOUNG OTTO
          ... Interest me, like...?

                    SONYA
          What kinds of things do you like to
          do? What are you passionate about?

                    YOUNG OTTO
               (He thinks a moment.)
          Machines. Engines. I like knowing
          how things work. What each part
          does to make a car run smoothly.
          It's more complicated than most
          people realize. A carburetor has to
          mix gas and air in just the right
          combination, then the spark plugs
          ignite that mixture and that drives
          the pistons which drive the
          connecting rods and the driveshaft -

Otto sees Sonya trying to follow what he's saying. He grows
self-conscious and trails off, shaking his head.

                    SONYA
          ... Where did you learn so much
          about cars?

                    YOUNG OTTO
          From my father. That's mostly all
          we talked about. He was a good dad,
          though. Dependable.

                    SONYA
          He passed away?

                    YOUNG OTTO
                (Nods.)
            Two months ago. It was sudden.

                    SONYA
            I'm sorry. And your mom?

                    YOUNG OTTO
            I don't remember her much. Just how
            it felt when she was gone.

Sonya's heart goes out to him. She watches him sip his soup.

                    SONYA
            Why didn't you get an entrée?

                    YOUNG OTTO
                (A pained confession:)
            ... I ate at home.

                    SONYA
            Why?

                    YOUNG OTTO
            So you could order what you wanted.
                (He sets his napkin down.)
            Look, I lied to you, I'm sorry. I'm
            not in the army - I couldn't pass
            my physical. If I had, at least I'd
            have a job now, that's what I was
            counting on. But now I don't and I
            don't know what I'm going to do -
                (He rises.)
            I should go...

Young Otto rises, about to excuse himself. Sonya stands, takes Otto by the wrist and pulls him into a kiss. Other diners laugh and applaud. As Fog envelopes the scene, the echoing applause morphs into a persistent banging noise...

                                        END FLASHBACK.

33   I/E. OTTO'S GARAGE/CHEVY MALIBU - DAY   33

Otto sits in his car, eyes closed, his hand on his wrist. The banging continues. He stirs, slowly realizing that someone is pounding on the garage door.

                    MARISOL (O.S.)
            Otto! Otto!

Exasperated, Otto turns off the car and climbs out, stumbling over the hose as he crosses to the garage door.

                    OTTO
          What, for God's sake?!

He throws the garage door open. Marisol scrambles backward to
avoid being hit by it.

                    MARISOL
          ¡¡Ay - mierda!! What are you doing
          in there?

Otto scrambles to close the garage door.

                    OTTO
               (Defensively:)
          What are you doing??

                    MARISOL
          Looking for you!

                    OTTO
          Well, you found me.

                    MARISOL
          I need you to take me to the
          hospital. Tommy fell off the
          ladder! The ambulance took him
          already.

                    OTTO
          Then you can drive yourself in that
          Japanese toaster you call a car.

                    MARISOL
          I don't have a license.

                    OTTO
               (Shocked:)
          What do you mean? How old are you?

                    MARISOL
          Thirty.

                    OTTO
          And you don't have a license?

                    MARISOL
          I got the permit. I just never
          learned the driving part.

                    OTTO
          How many other parts are there?

Marisol groans, snapping her fingers in Otto's face.

MARISOL
¡Oye! ¡Escúchame - focus! Tommy may be dying! Are you going to drive me to the hospital or are you going to make me take the bus?

OTTO
No - I'll drive you!

MARISOL
At last! Was that so hard?

Marisol heads off toward her house.

OTTO
Where are you going?

MARISOL
To get the children.

OTTO
The CHILDREN??

34 I/E. OTTO'S CHEVY MALIBU - DAY 34

Otto has pulled his car out of the garage and now covers the backseat with newspaper, fanning the door open and shut to clear out the smell of exhaust.

Marisol returns with the kids, carrying a car seat for Abbie. Luna carries her booster seat and a pair of action figures.

ABBIE
Hi, "O-t-t-o."

MARISOL
Get in back, girls.

Marisol opens the back door to put Abbie's car seat in, sees the newspaper covering the seats. She grimaces, sets the car seat on top of the newspaper and buckles Abbie in.

MARISOL (CONT'D)
There you go, *pajarito*.

OTTO
(As he climbs in:)
Can't believe your parents never taught you to drive.

MARISOL
My mother never learned. My father never got the chance.

Marisol closes Abbie's door and opens the passenger door. She pointedly shoves the paper off her own seat and climbs in.

>   ABBIE
>   It smells stinky in here!

>   LUNA
>   Seriously, Mom, I can't breathe.

Marisol becomes fully aware of the stench in the cabin.

>   MARISOL
>   Roll down the windows.

They do so.

>   OTTO
>   No, come on. It's freezing out.

Marisol turns on the heat, turns pointedly to Otto.

>   MARISOL
>   What were you doing in there?

>   OTTO
>   (Shutting the heater off:)
>   The windows are open! May as well
>   try heating the whole outdoors.

Otto takes off the parking brake and puts the car in gear, avoiding Marisol's gaze.

35	OMITTED	35
36	EXT. HOSPITAL ENTRANCE - DAY	36

ESTABLISHING: the entrance of a hospital emergency room.

37	OMITTED	37
38	INT. HOSPITAL FAMILY WAITING ROOM - DAY	38

Otto sits awkwardly on a low couch in a waiting room, watching as Luna plays with her action figure dolls - two *Lucha Libre* wrestlers - on the floor nearby.

>   OTTO
>   Those dolls - are they Superheroes?

                          LUNA
                Luchadoros - wrestlers. Yah!

Luna has one of her dolls pick up the other one and slam him against the wall. Otto reacts, surprised.

Abbie charges over to Otto carrying a children's book.

                          ABBIE
                I found a Mr. Bear book!

                          OTTO
                Yes, I can see that.

                          LUNA
                She wants you to read it to her.

Otto reluctantly takes the book. Abbie sits beside him. A beat, then Otto begins reading:

                          OTTO
                "Where, oh where, is my Baby Bear-"

                          ABBIE
                No - talk like a bear! "Grrr..."

                          OTTO
                Bears don't talk.

                          LUNA
                This one does.

Otto stares at the book, growls a little, finds a bear voice.

                          OTTO
                "Are you there, Baby Bear, up in
                that tree?"

                          ABBIE
                No - it's an owl!

                          OTTO
                    (He nods, encouraged,
                     tries an owl voice.)
                "There's nobody here but baby and
                me!"
                    (Back to the bear voice:)
                Are you there, Baby Bear, deep
                underground?"

BEPPO THE CLOWN enters the waiting room full clown makeup and outfit.

                    BEPPO
               (Playfully, arms wide:)
          I'm no Baby Bear! I'm Beppo!

The girls jump off the couch, excited.

                    LUNA
          Hello, Beppo!

                    BEPPO
          Would you like to see a trick?

                    ABBIE
          Yes!

                    OTTO
               (Annoyed:)
          I was actually reading to them.

                    BEPPO
          'I was actually reading to them,'
          Mr. Bear grumbled. Say, can I
          borrow a coin, Mr. Bear?

Otto looks to the girls, pats his pockets. No change. Beat.
He reaches into his shirt pocket, pulls out the quarter.

                    OTTO
          I need this back.

A SHORT TIME LATER - Marisol comes back into family waiting
room. Luna and Abbie are waiting there alone.

                    MARISOL
          Where's Otto?

39   EXT. HOSPITAL ENTRANCE - DAY   39

Marisol and the children go outside. Otto is in the midst of
a standoff confrontation with two HOSPITAL SECURITY OFFICERS.

                    MARISOL
          Otto! What the hell did you do?

                    OTTO
          Nothing!

                    ABBIE
               (Giggling:)
          Abuelo Otto hit the clown!

                    OTTO
          I did not!

LUNA
(Laughing:)
Abuelo Luchadoro!

OTTO
(Indignant:)
It was all that clown's fault!

FLASH BACK TO:

40   I/E. HOSPITAL FAMILY WAITING ROOM/HALLWAY (FLASHBACK) - DAY   40

NOTE: the waiting room has a glass observation window that looks out into the hallway. Portions of the following scene will be shot looking into the room through the observation window.

Beppo pulls a coin out of his ear, delighting the girls.

BEPPO
Wow! Here it is!

He hands the coin back to Otto. Otto looks at it, rises.

OTTO
Hang on - this isn't my quarter.

BEPPO
What? Yes it is.

Otto shows the edge of the quarter to Beppo.

OTTO
No, it isn't. You see that? Copper and nickel. Mine is silver, 1964 -

He points toward Beppo's colorful, oversized patch pocket.

OTTO (CONT'D)
And it's still right there in your pocket.

BEPPO
(Lowering his voice:)
What's wrong with you?

OTTO
Nothing! I just want my own quarter back, that's all!

BEPPO
(Nodding to the girls:)
I feel sorry for them.

                    OTTO
          Give me the - !

Otto grabs at Beppo's pocket, inadvertently stepping on one
of the clown's shoes. Beppo tries to pull away and his pocket
rips off in Otto's hand. The clown loses his balance and goes
down hard. Otto's coin falls to the floor, spinning to rest.

                                        END FLASHBACK.

41   INT. OTTO'S CHEVY MALIBU, HOSPITAL PARKING LOT - DAY   41

Otto, Marisol and the girls climb into Otto's car in silence.
Otto pulls out his keys - along with Beppo's patch pocket,
which he tosses on the dash. Marisol stares at the pocket as
Otto starts the car, then begins laughing quietly to herself.

                    OTTO
               (Grumpily:)
          What?

Marisol shakes her head, tries to stop laughing.

                    MARISOL
          My father used to smile like that.

                    OTTO
               (He starts the car.)
          I'm not smiling.

                    MARISOL
          Exactly.

Otto looks back toward the hospital, growing impatient.

                    OTTO
          Where's Alvin Wrench? Is he coming
          or - ?

                    LUNA
          He's right there at the front door.

Otto looks in the rearview mirror. Tommy is sitting in a
wheelchair in front of the building, one leg in a cast that
extends straight out in front of him. He waves, fumbles for
crutches, tries to rise.

                    MARISOL
          Pull the car around - we'll pick
          him up.

| 42 | I/E. OTTO'S GARAGE - DAY | 42 |

The Chevy Malibu comes to a stop in front of Otto's garage. Tommy sits in the back between the two girls, his broken leg propped up on the console between the front seats.

> TOMMY
> Hey, Otto, you think maybe you could drop me off in front of our house?

> OTTO
> You're going to have to get used to those crutches sometime.

> TOMMY
> Yeah, I suppose I will.

Otto, Marisol and the girls climb out. Luna takes her booster seat out and leaves the seat forward for Tommy to get out behind her. Marisol comes around to the other side of the car to help.

> MARISOL
> (To Otto:)
> Thank you for driving.

Otto nods, grunts. He takes a few steps toward the garage, stops. Marisol notices Otto, glances to the garage, and stops, remembering. Tommy continues to struggle to get out of the car behind them, unnoticed.

> MARISOL (CONT'D)
> Well... bye then.

Otto nods, doesn't turn. Abbie hurries over to Otto, giving his leg a hug. Luna follows, hugging him as well.

> ABBIE
> Bye, *Abuelo*.

> LUNA
> Bye... *Abuelo Luchadoro*.

The girls laugh. Otto almost smiles. Tommy appears on crutches, having made it out of the car.

> TOMMY
> Thanks again, Otto.

Otto nods, hurrying the girls off toward their father. Marisol stays behind a beat longer.

MARISOL
You know, I think our radiator
needs looking at, too. Could you do
it?
    (With a smile:)
I don't want my girls to freeze
tonight. I mean, it's bad enough
they had to watch you attack a
clown.

OTTO
    (Beat. He shrugs.)
All right. Why not? This crappy day
is ruined anyway.

43 EXT. OTTO'S HOUSE - MORNING 43

It is lightly snowing. Otto shovels. He pauses, hearing the sound of a car starting, sees the Dye & Merica car drive toward the gate at the end of the street. Otto tosses the shovel aside and gives chase, slamming his hand on the trunk of the car as it tries to pull up over the curb.

OTTO
HEY!

The car stops. The Dye & Merica Agent gets out of the car.

OTTO (CONT'D)
What do I have to do?! Put tire
spikes in the grass?!

The Agent gives Otto a friendly smile as he approaches.

DYE & MERICA AGENT
Otto Anderson - "the man who won't
budge."

OTTO
    (Surprised:)
How do you know my name?

DYE & MERICA AGENT
You're a local legend. I hear
you've been holding up development
on this street for years.
    (Conciliatory:)
Look, I don't want to tangle with
you, Otto. But I have to do my job.

OTTO
You call that a job? Coercing
people into selling their homes?

The Agent shakes his head, heads back toward his car.

                    OTTO (CONT'D)
          Don't you dare drive that car on
          the grass!

                    DYE & MERICA AGENT
          Just to be clear, Otto: my company
          bought this house - this is *our*
          grass. We own most of these other
          houses too. They're private
          property. I can do whatever I want.

The Agent climbs in his car, starts the engine. Otto slams his hand on the car's hood, furious.

                    OTTO
          You son of a bitch! You think - !

Otto tenses abruptly, getting chest pains. The car drives off. Otto sinks to one knee, fighting off the pain. He waits for the pain to subside, slowly wills himself to his feet.

As Otto limps toward his house, he hears Marisol cry out:

                    MARISOL (O.S.)
          ¡Ay no! ¡Que tristesa!

Otto watches as Marisol hurries down her front steps to a snowdrift next to her porch. He goes over to investigate. The Mangy Cat lies in the snow drift, its fur covered in ice.

                    MARISOL (CONT'D)
          Is he dead?

                    OTTO
              (He shrugs.)
          Maybe he's sleeping.

                    MARISOL
          You have to get him out of there!

                    OTTO
          Why can't you?

                    MARISOL
          I'm pregnant! I'm not supposed to
          handle cats. I could get toxo-
          something.

                    OTTO
          Well, he got himself in there; he
          should be able to get himself out.

                    MARISOL
          Dios Mío, what's wrong with you?

                    OTTO
          Nothing. I've just never gotten
          along with cats is all.

Jimmy power-walks up to them in his sweat suit.

                    JIMMY
          Hey man, what's going on?
               (Peering into the drift:)
          Whoa! We got to warm you up, buddy!

He reaches into the snow and pulls out an icy blob of fur.
Marisol grabs Jimmy's arm, marching him to Otto's house.

                    MARISOL
          Otto! Open the damn door!

44   INT. OTTO'S HOUSE - DAY   44

Jimmy brushes lumps of snow off of the cat as they go inside.

                    OTTO
          Stop that! You're getting snow all
          over the floor!

                    MARISOL
          My God, its freezing in here!

Marisol notices the women's coats that line the hall and
starts looking through them for something to warm the cat.

                    OTTO
          No, no - *leave those alone!*

                    MARISOL
          Then get a blanket.

                    OTTO
          A blanket? For the <u>cat</u>?

                    MARISOL
          For the <u>frozen</u> cat - yes!

                    JIMMY
          I got this.

Jimmy unzips the front of his sweat suit and stuffs the cat
inside it, pressed to his bare skin.

50.

                    OTTO
          What in God's name are you doing?

                    JIMMY
          Body heat - works wonders. And I
          got plenty, body and heat.

                    OTTO
          You're going to smother him in
          there. I can't even see his head.

                    MARISOL
               (Heading for the kitchen:)
          I'm turning the oven on.

                    OTTO
          You're not putting that cat in my
          oven!

                    MARISOL
          Of course not! I'm trying to get
          some heat in this house!

                    OTTO
          No, no - stay out of my kitchen!

45   OMITTED   45

46   OMITTED   46

47   INT. OTTO'S KITCHEN - CONTINUOUS   47

Marisol enters and looks around, surprised. The counters are
all much lower than standard ones. Otto appears behind her.

                    MARISOL
          Your counters are so low! Mine, I
          feel like I'm chopping onions right
          under my chin. These are perfect.
          Where did you get them?

                    OTTO
          I made them. For Sonya. My wife.

                    MARISOL
          Okay. Is she here or...?

Jimmy steps into in the doorway behind Otto. He pulls the
Cat, which seems to be reviving, out of his shirt.

                    JIMMY
          Sonya passed away. She was a great
          cook, though, wasn't she? I used to
          eat here all the time.

                    MARISOL
               (To Otto:)
          I'm sorry.

                    OTTO
               (A stiff nod.)
          Can we please get out of my kitchen
          now? I've got things to do.

     He grabs his car keys, shuffles everyone toward the door.
     Jimmy turns, lifting the Cat up into Otto's face.

                    JIMMY
          Who's going to look after this guy?

                    OTTO
               (Waving Jimmy away:)
          You are. Go on - time to go.

     Marisol, Jimmy and the Cat leave and Otto shuts the door
     firmly behind them. He stands for a moment in silence then
     turns, looking around his empty house, remembering...

48   EXT. LUCAS'S FARMHOUSE, DRIVEWAY 1976 (MEMORY) - DAY   48

     Sonya picks up a chubby barn cat (ERNEST) and holds it out
     affectionately toward Young Otto, nearly pressing their faces
     together.

                    SONYA
          This is Ernest, my guard dog. Say
          hello to Otto.

                    YOUNG OTTO
          ... Hello.

     They are standing in the dirt driveway outside a rural
     farmhouse. A screen door creaks - Sonya turns as LUCAS (50s),
     Sonya's taciturn father, comes out of the house.

                    SONYA
          Hey, Daddy!

     Sony puts Ernest down and hurries forward to hug her father.
     Ernest goes onto the porch to eat food from the same colorful
     bowl that Otto finds in his cupboard years later. Young Otto
     hangs back a moment as Sonya and Lucas greet one another.

                    SONYA (CONT'D)
          You got rid of the beard.

                              LUCAS
                    (Slight Swedish accent:)
                  Got tired of not shaving.

Sonya steps back, turns to Young Otto.

                              SONYA
                  Dad, this is Otto.

                              LUCAS
                  All right, then.

                              YOUNG OTTO
                  Hello.

Pause. Otto's eyes wander nervously away from Lucas's, falling on the pickup in the driveway. Otto notices the logo on the truck - Chevy - and visibly relaxes.

                              YOUNG OTTO (CONT'D)
                  That's a Silverado C20, right?
                  Camper Special?

                              LUCAS
                  It is.

                              YOUNG OTTO
                  Well, that's a fine truck. Did you
                  get the automatic transmission?

                              LUCAS
                  Nope. Never saw the need for one.

                              YOUNG OTTO
                  Neither have I, sir. Not if you
                  know how to drive.

                              LUCAS
                    (A nod.)
                  Uses a lot of gas, though. And the
                  engine's been acting up lately.
                  Doesn't sound right.

                              YOUNG OTTO
                  You mind if I have a look?

49   OMITTED   49

50   INT. LUCAS'S BARN/TRUCK (MEMORY) - DUSK   50

Young Otto looks under the hood of the truck, which Lucas has pulled into his barn. He goes into the cab, starts the engine, listens as the engine sputters, then turns the engine off and climbs out.

                    YOUNG OTTO
               The timing needs to be adjusted.
               And you might need hotter plugs.
               That'll cut down on how much gas
               you're burning. I can take care of
               that for you.

Sonya walks up the driveway and peers into the barn, watching as the two men talk.

                    LUCAS
               Have you ever thought about opening
               your own repair shop?

                    YOUNG OTTO
                    (Closing the hood:)
               I have. Sonya's been talking to me
               about taking some engineering
               courses. I might give that a try.

                    LUCAS
               All right, then.

Lucas turns and walks a few steps ahead of Young Otto on his way out of the barn, glancing at Sonya as he passes her.

                    LUCAS (CONT'D)
               He had better learn to fish.

He leaves. Young Otto approaches Sonya. She hugs him, elated.

                    SONYA
               He likes you.

                              END MEMORY/FLASHBACK.

51   I/E. CHEVY MALIBU, TRAIN STATION PARKING LOT, 2018 - DAY   51

Otto (60s) sits in his car in the station parking lot, remembering. Outside, it has stopped snowing. Otto hears a train approach, glances up, watching as COMMUTERS file into the parking lot....

                                        MATCH CUT TO:

52   EXT. COLLEGE AUDITORIUM/PARKING LOT, 1978 (MEMORY) - DAY   52

Elated COLLEGE GRADS go out to their cars in their graduation robes. A banner reads "CONGRATULATIONS CLASS of '78. *Young Otto* and Sonya are in the crowd, Otto in a robe.

53   I/E. CHEVY CHEVETTE, 1978 (MEMORY) - DAY   53

Young Otto and Sonya get in Otto's car. Sonya opens Young Otto's diploma.

                    SONYA
          "The Board of Regents hereby
          certifies that Otto Anderson..."

Young Otto grows serious. He lowers his eyes. On Sonya:

                    SONYA (CONT'D)
          "Having completed all the
          requirements for a Bachelor's
          Degree in Engineering -"

                    YOUNG OTTO (O.S.)
          Would you ever... ?

54   INT. CHEVY MALIBU, TRAIN STATION PARKING LOT, 2018 - DAY   54

Otto (60s) finishes Young Otto's sentence.

                    OTTO
          ... Want to get married?

Silence. PAN OVER TO REVEAL Sonya in the Chevy Malibu beside Otto. She turns to him, surprised. Otto doesn't look at her.

                    OTTO (CONT'D)
          Because I was thinking if... I
          wondered if you might want us to...
          because if you did...

                    SONYA
          Take a breath, Otto. Look at me.
               (He does so.)
          Now... Ask me the right way.

                    OTTO
          Will you - ?

55   I/E. PARKING LOT/OTTO'S CHEVETTE, 1978 (MEMORY) - CONTINUOUS   55

The question is interrupted as excited grads storm past the car, hooting and banging on the hood, which sets off a chorus of cars honking.

Young Otto looks around, startled. Sonya bursts out laughing. He asks again, his voice nearly drowned out by all the noise.

                    YOUNG OTTO
              Will you marry me?

                    SONYA
              Yes!

The honking and hooting and banging continues as the couple
kiss and embrace. Sonya honks Otto's car horn, laughing. The
car horn morphs into a TRAIN HORN...

56   I/E. CHEVY MALIBU/ TRAIN STATION PARKING LOT, 2018 - DAY   56

Otto (60s), alone in his Chevy Malibu, looks up as a train
departs. He gets out of the car, walks toward the station.

57   EXT. OTTO'S TRAIN STATION, 2018 - DAY   57

Otto comes up the steps and makes his way through COMMUTERS
to the edge of the platform. Another horn. Otto looks up the
track. The next train is coming. Otto braces himself to jump.

Further along the platform, a BUSINESSMAN suddenly collapses
and tumbles off onto the tracks, unconscious. People cry out -

                    COMMUTERS
              Oh my God! / He fell on the tracks!
              / Someone help him! *(etc.)*

One COMMUTER calls 911; another records the event on her
phone. Otto realizes no one is actually going to help him.

                    OTTO
              Oh, for God's sake -

Otto glances to the rapidly approaching train, then jumps
down onto the track and strains to lift the businessman,
dragging him to the edge of the platform.

                    OTTO (CONT'D)
              Someone give me a goddamn hand!

Several commuters help Otto lift the man up onto the platform
and everyone cheers.

Otto realizes everyone is focused on the unconscious man - no
one is looking his way. He hears the train sound its horn and
turns, watching as it rapidly closes in.

Otto closes his eyes, preparing for the impact, then hears
Sonya's voice in his mind, the sound of the train fading...

                    SONYA (V.O.)
            That's enough now, darling...

Otto opens his eyes, sees the train rushing toward him. A
BURLY COMMUTER leans out over the platform's edge, calling:

                    BURLY COMMUTER
            Take my hand! Take my hand, now!

A MOTHER with THREE CHILDREN watch on in horror. Otto meets
eyes with her YOUNGEST DAUGHTER - then takes the Commuter's
hand and climbs to safety just before the train rushes past.

Otto winces as he rises, pushing back pain. The Burly
Commuter eyes Otto as though he's crazy -

                    BURLY COMMUTER (CONT'D)
            Are you out of your mind?

But everyone else cheers, congratulating Otto and slapping
him on the back. Otto wants nothing to do with any of it. He
walks stiffly to the stairs and heads for the parking lot.

58   INT. OTTO'S MALIBU, 2018/ CHEVETTE, 1980 (MEMORY) -   58
        DAY/INTERCUT

Otto drives past chain restaurants, big box stores and strip
malls. He notices an old Sears store, now closed for good,
and remembers...

... The same roadside, almost completely undeveloped save for
the Sears store.

59   I/E. OTTO'S MALIBU/OTTO AND SONYA'S HOUSE, 1980 (MEMORY) - 59
        CONTINUOUS

OTTO'S CHEVY MALIBU (2018) drives down a quiet street.

                    SONYA (V.O.)
            That must be it - on the left.

The Malibu slows and turns onto Birchwood Drive, a quiet
street surrounded by woods. The center meridian is dotted
with flowerbeds and saplings.

Otto (60s) stops in front of what will soon be their home, a
FOR SALE sign out front. He eyes the house critically.

                    OTTO
            I don't know. You can't always
            trust the construction in these new
            developments -

SONYA
          I love it!

Sonya jumps out of the car and hurries up the front walk.
Otto climbs out, calling after her.

                    OTTO
          Okay. But we don't want to tip our
          hand too much, so don't -

The REALTOR comes onto the porch to greet Sonya.

                    SONYA
          I love it!

Off Otto's reaction:
                                              CUT TO:

A trailer parks perfectly in front of their new home. Sonya
and *Young Otto* get out of the car and open the trailer.

WIDE ANGLE as YOUNG ANITA and YOUNG REUBEN (both late 20s)
come over to greet the new neighbors, Young Anita carrying a
casserole dish.

Within moments, the women exchange hugs and chat away like
old friends as they head off into the house, leaving Young
Otto and Young Reuben standing in awkward silence.

                    YOUNG REUBEN
          Can I help you unpack the trailer?

                    YOUNG OTTO
          That's okay.

                    YOUNG REUBEN
          You sure?

                    YOUNG OTTO
          Yeah. Thanks, though.

                    YOUNG REUBEN
          Okay.
              (Pause.)
          Here's the thing, though. Anita
          told me I had to help you, so if I
          don't, I'm going to hear about it.

                    YOUNG OTTO
          Okay.

As they start toward the trailer, a motorcycle speeds past.
The two both instinctively give chase, shouting:

                    YOUNG OTTO / YOUNG REUBEN
               Hey! Slow down!

They stop at the end of the street, incensed, then look at
one another, realizing they might have more in common than
they thought.

60   EXT. OTTO'S HOUSE/NEIGHBORHOOD 1980 (MEMORY) - DAY/MONTAGE   60

        GOOD NEIGHBORS MONTAGE:

        - SIDEWALK: Sonya and Young Anita come outside to help the
          men unpack the trailer, both noticing the uncharacteristic
          chattiness of their husbands.

        - LIVING ROOM: Young Otto and Young Reuben enter carrying
          boxes. Young Otto sends Young Reuben into the kitchen and
          sets his box down, turning as Sonya enters *(This is the
          scene in which Otto says he'll build another bookcase)*.

        - RECYCLING AREA: Young Reuben shows Otto where to put used
          boxes and how to use the reach extender tool to sort glass.

        - GARAGE: Young Otto gives Reuben a tour of his workbench,
          demonstrating the right way to sharpen a handsaw.

        Young Reuben leads Young Otto over to his garage, raises
        his garage door and shows off his table saw - but all Young
        Otto sees is the brand logo on Young Reuben's car... <u>FORD</u>.

                                         END MEMORY/ FLASHBACK.

61   I/E. OTTO'S CHEVY MALIBU, 2018 - DAY   61

        Otto (60s) sits outside his garage in his Chevy Malibu.

                    OTTO
               I should have known then.

        Someone taps at his window. Otto looks over, startled.
        Marisol is outside the car, smiling. Otto climbs out.

                    OTTO (CONT'D)
               Are you trying to scare me to
               death?

                    MARISOL
               (Handing Otto a drawing:)
               Look at this: Abbie drew a picture
               of her new neighbors. She wanted
               you to have it. That's you there -
               she always draws you in color.

OTTO
What do you mean 'always?'

MARISOL
(Ignoring this:)
Listen, I had a great idea. You can be my driving instructor.

OTTO
No, I don't have time for that.

MARISOL
Don't worry - I'll pay for the gas -

Jimmy comes down the street with a cardboard box which seems to be moving. Yowling and clawing sounds come from inside it.

JIMMY
There you guys are! I've been looking for you everywhere.

MARISOL
Jimmy, what are you doing?

OTTO
What the hell? Is the cat in there?

The clawing becomes more furious.

JIMMY
Yeah - jeez, calm down, dude! He really doesn't like this -

OTTO
Then let him out!

Jimmy opens the box. The cat leaps out, hissing. It struts over behind Otto and sits, glaring back at Jimmy.

JIMMY
Sorry, buddy.

OTTO
What did you think you were doing? Taking him for a walk?

Jimmy gives a sheepish smile and pulls his collar aside, revealing a nasty red rash on his neck and chest.

JIMMY
I forgot I'm allergic.

Marisol grabs Jimmy's arm and hurries him toward her house.

MARISOL
Oh, my God! Come with me - Tommy got a prescription last year after he found a wasp's nest.

OTTO
Wait - what about the cat?

JIMMY
Looks like he's yours now, Otto!

Marisol and Jimmy disappear inside. Off Otto's reaction -

CUT TO:

62 EXT. CEMETERY - DAY 62

Otto removes the old flowers from Sonya's grave, replacing them with fresh flowers.

OTTO
I'm sorry I haven't come yet. It's been harder than I thought, killing myself. And now he's moved in...

Otto glances over as the Cat pops its head out of the cardboard box, which sits beside the gravestone.

OTTO (CONT'D)
You'd probably want to keep him. You always liked cats. But I want to be here with you. I just need to figure out what to do with him first, then I'll join you, Sonya.
(Pressing his hand to Sonya's gravestone:)
I miss you.

The cat comes forward. It rubs its back along the underside of Otto's arm, then gently rests its head against his palm.

63 INT. OTTO'S BATHROOM/BEDROOM - NIGHT 63

Otto finishes brushing his teeth, comes out of his bathroom in pajamas and robe. He finds the Cat splayed out on his bed.

OTTO
You're not taking over my bed!

Otto picks up the Cat, setting him on a towel near the door.

                    OTTO (CONT'D)
          That's your bed - got it?
                (The Cat stares at him.)
          Would you rather sleep out in the
          snow? No, I didn't think so.

Otto goes to close the blinds, pausing to look at the drawing
Abbie drew of him, which sits on his bedside table.

                    SONYA (O.S.)
          I didn't think you liked children.

Sonya, reflected in the window, passes behind Otto and goes
into the bathroom to brush her teeth.

                    OTTO
          I don't 'not' like children. I'm
          just not sure if I'd be a very good
          dad. All I ever learned from my own
          dad was how to fix engines and cook
          potatoes.

                    SONYA (O.S.)
          That's all you need to do.

                    OTTO
          Is it? I don't know. We ate a lot
          of potatoes.

                    SONYA
                (Re-enters, smiling:)
          You'll be the best dad our children
          could ever hope for.

64   INT. OTTO'S BEDROOM (2018) - MORNING   64

Otto awakens the next morning. The Cat is splayed out next to
him, sound asleep. Otto holds the Cat's tail in his palm.

65   INT. OTTO'S DINING ROOM/KITCHEN - DAY   65

Otto puts cat food into the colorful bowl, then sets out two
coffee cups, pours. As the Cat eats, Otto sits, raises his
coffee in a toast and takes a sip, then turns to gaze out the
window...

                                        MEMORY/FLASH BACK TO:

| 66 | I/E. LUCAS'S FARMHOUSE, 1981 (MEMORY) - EVENING | 66 |

INSIDE - a Coroner's van and a police car can be seen through the front window of the farmhouse.

OUTSIDE in the yard, the CORONER talks with a grieving Sonya and *Young Otto*. A POLICE OFFICER stands nearby, listening in.

Up on the porch, Ernest the cat checks his bowl for food. It's empty.

| 67 | I/E. OTTO AND SONYA'S HOUSE, 1981 (MEMORY) - DUSK | 67 |

It is getting dark outside. Young Otto takes a clear shotgun case and fishing rod out of a trailer hitched to his car.

He goes to his front door and puts the rod and case inside, then comes back out. Sonya sits on a bench on the porch, staring out into the night, her features cloaked in shadow.

     YOUNG OTTO
  You doing okay?

Sonya nods. Beat. She shakes her head.

     SONYA
  You're going to have to love me
  twice as much now, Otto.

     YOUNG OTTO
  I don't know if that's even
  possible, but I'll try.

He goes to sit beside Sonya - but Ernest the cat has taken that seat and now stares up at Otto, lips curled in disgust.

     YOUNG OTTO (CONT'D)
  That cat of yours doesn't like me.

Sonya nudges Ernest off the bench.

     SONYA
  He's just jealous. Give him time.
  You'll have to take care of him -
  at least until the baby comes.

Otto (60s) now sits beside Sonya taking in this news.

     OTTO
  Baby? Really?

SONYA
(Nods, fights emotion.)
I wanted to tell you and Dad
together.

Otto pulls Sonya close, gazes off in thought.

OTTO
We'll need to buy a station wagon.
The Caprice Classic.

SONYA
And maybe a crib.

OTTO
No - I'll make you one. And I'll
look after the cat for you.

68   EXT. OTTO'S HOUSE/STREET, 2018 - MORNING   68

Malcolm comes down the street on the bike, tossing ad flyers
in front of houses. Otto appears out of nowhere, grabbing the
bike by the handlebars. Malcolm barely stops in time.

OTTO
Hey!

MALCOLM
What are you doing?!

Otto grabs a flyer out of the bag at Malcolm's hip.

OTTO
This is what you use the bike for?

MALCOLM
Yeah, it's my job.

OTTO
No, no - a job is waiting tables or
pumping gas.

MALCOLM
I also work nights in a pizza shop
and weekends at a thrift store, so -

OTTO
You do?

Malcolm nods, defiant - then looks over at Otto's house.

MALCOLM
You're Mr. Anderson, aren't you?
You used to come to the
presentations at school.

OTTO
What of it?

MALCOLM
Mrs. Anderson was my teacher. She
was the first person who didn't
treat me like a freak because I'm
transgender. She was the first to
call me by my new name and she got
the other teachers to do it, too.
That really helped me at school.
    (Takes the flyer back.)
I won't leave these here anymore.

Malcolm starts to ride off. Otto gazes after him, stunned.

OTTO
Hey! What is your name?

MALCOLM
Malcolm.

OTTO
    (Beat. A curt nod.)
Okay. I'm Otto.

MALCOLM
    (As he goes:)
Nice to meet you, Otto.

A Toyota Camry comes up beside Otto and lurches to a perilous
halt. Marisol rolls down the window; Andy sits next to her.

MARISOL
Good news! Andy is going to give me
driving lessons before work!

ANDY
Same time tomorrow, then?

MARISOL
Yes - thank you!

Marisol climbs out of the car. The Camry begins to roll away.

OTTO
Park!

                    MARISOL
            What?

                    OTTO
            The car's still in drive! It's
            automatic! You've got to put it in
            park!

Too late. They watch the Camry roll off, screeching to a halt when Andy finally manages to climb over and hit the brake. On Otto as he imagines Marisol's next driving lesson...

69 OMITTED   69

70 OMITTED   70

71 I/E. MARISOL & TOMMY'S FRONT PORCH/OTTO'S FORD - DAY   71

Otto steps up onto the porch, knocks. Tommy answers the door. He wears a *Lucha Libra* wrestling mask pushed up on his head and has a towel tucked into the back of his shirt as a cape. Luna, beside Tommy, has her own cape and the wrestling dolls.

                    TOMMY
            Hi, Otto.

Otto squints, nonplussed. He sees Marisol in the hallway behind Tommy and leans to one side to talk to her.

                    OTTO
            Get your coat. Lesson time.
                (Holding up his car keys:)
            I can't stand watching one idiot
            trying to teach another how to
            drive.

Marisol hurries forward gives Otto a hug, delighted.

                    MARISOL
            Really? Oh, thank you - I'll be
            right out! I have to cancel Andy!

She hurries back inside.

                    TOMMY
            That's seriously nice of you, man.

Otto looks at Tommy, tries to think of a response, can't. He turns and walks out to his car, which is parked at the curb.

MINUTES LATER, Marisol bounds outside carrying a Tupperware container. Otto waits for her by his car.

MARISOL
I brought you more *salpors*!
          (She looks at the car and
          slows, growing anxious:)
Can't we use our car, though?
I've only ever driven automatic.

Otto takes the cookies and opens the passenger side door.

OTTO
Then you don't know how to drive.

72 OMITTED   72

73 I/E. OTTO'S CHEVY MALIBU/LOCAL STREET - DAY   73

The car lurches down the street toward an intersection.

OTTO
Okay, the light's red up there, so
you need to slow down. Push down on
the clutch. The clutch - yes, good.
Now the brake. No - leave the
clutch in. And brake - brake!

MARISOL
Stop shouting at me!

OTTO
I'm not shouting!

Otto yanks on the parking brake. The car screeches to a halt inches from the car in front of them. Both take deep breaths.

MARISOL
I suck at this.

OTTO
No, you're learning.

MARISOL
I nearly hit that car.

OTTO
Doesn't matter. It's a hybrid.

MARISOL
I should back up.

OTTO
Don't. You're fine where you are.

Otto glances in the side mirror. An oversized pickup truck driven by NICK (20s, a musclehead) has pulled up close behind them. The light turns green. Otto releases the parking brake.

OTTO (CONT'D)
Okay, green light. Now ease off the clutch and give it some gas.

Marisol does so. The engine revs. The car doesn't move. Nick lays on the horn. Marisol begins to panic.

OTTO (CONT'D)
You're not in gear. You need to put it in first.

The engine makes a horrific grinding noise, dies. Marisol turns the key. The engine coughs. Nick honks.

OTTO (CONT'D)
Stop turning the key. Press in the clutch.

Nick honks, then rolls forward, nudging the back of Otto's car with his oversized bumper. Marisol bursts into tears. Otto glances back toward the pickup truck, furious.

MARISOL
I can't do it!

OTTO
God damn it...

Otto climbs out of the car, marching back to the driver's side window of the pickup, glaring.

OTTO (CONT'D)
What's wrong with you? She's just learning! Did you never have to learn to drive?

NICK
Calm it down, old man.

OTTO
Old man? I'm not your old man, you stupid son of a bitch -

Otto rips open the pickup door, yanking Nick out and pinning him against the truck. Nick freezes, surprised by Otto's strength and the intensity of his anger.

                    OTTO (CONT'D)
          If you honk that goddamn horn
          again, it will be the last thing
          you ever do! You got that? Huh?

Beat. Nick lowers his eyes. Otto lets him go and walks away, returning to his own car.

Marisol stares at Otto as he gets in, mouth agape. Otto closes the car door, buckles in, then turns to Marisol, speaking with deliberate calm.

                    OTTO (CONT'D)
          Now, you listen to me. You've given
          birth to two children - three soon
          enough. You came here all the way
          from another country, probably to
          get away from war and persecution
          and God knows what other kinds of
          hell. You learned a new language,
          you got yourself an education and a
          nitwit husband, and now you're
          holding that family together - so
          you will have no problem learning
          how to drive. I mean, we're not
          talking about brain surgery here.
          The world is full of complete
          idiots who've managed to figure it
          out. You are not a complete idiot.

Marisol takes this in. The light turns green.

                    OTTO (CONT'D)
          Now, drive.

Beat. Marisol shifts into gear, gently releases the clutch and accelerates. The car moves smoothly off down the road.

74   I/E. OTTO'S CHEVY MALIBU/STREET OUTSIDE A PASTRY SHOP - DAY   74

A short while later. Marisol pulls Otto's car to a stop just past an open parking spot on the street.

INSIDE THE CAR, Marisol looks absolutely terrified.

                    OTTO
          Look over your right shoulder and
          back up until your side mirror is
          in line with that car's bumper.

Marisol takes a breath, looks back, eases off the clutch.

MARISOL
Okay - okay... I'm there.

OTTO
Now turn sharply to the right and back up toward the curb... Good... Once as you've cleared that car's bumper, turn all the way left... now straighten out... And stop.

Marisol stops, shifts into first, pulls the parking brake and shuts the engine off.

MARISOL
Is that it?

OTTO
That's it.

Relieved, Marisol bursts out laughing - then finds herself fighting back tears. She shakes her head, embarrassed. Otto looks away, checks his watch, unbuckles his seatbelt.

OTTO (CONT'D)
And we're right on time.

MARISOL
For what?

75 INT. PASTRY SHOP AND CAFE - DAY   75

Otto carries a tray with pastries and coffee over to a table where Marisol waits. He sets out two cream-filled buns, sits.

OTTO
This is semlor - it's a Swedish eclair. Go ahead, try it.

Marisol takes a bite. Otto takes one as well, savoring it. He nods to Marisol (*good, eh*)? Marisol nods in agreement.

MARISOL
My God! Amazing! How did you find this place?

OTTO
Sonya found it. We used to come here every Saturday at one.

MARISOL
Then what?

OTTO
Go home at two. I'd wax the car.
Sonya would grade papers, cook.
Spend the rest of the day reading.

MARISOL
What kinds of books?

OTTO
(Shrugs:)
Books. I tried reading some of
them; it wasn't for me.
(Beat.)
Sonya's friends used to say we were
night and day. Everything in my
world was black and white until I
met Sonya. She was the color.

MARISOL
I would have liked her.

OTTO
(Nods:)
She was a force of nature.
Convinced the school to start a
program for kids who needed extra
help. A lot of them had problems at
home, social anxieties. By the time
she was done, they were reciting
Shakespeare. I ran into one of her
kids this morning -

Otto pauses, struck by an unexpected wave of emotion. He pushes it quickly aside and rises, grabbing his coffee cup.

OTTO (CONT'D)
You want more cream or - ?

MARISOL
I'm good, thanks.

Marisol watches Otto as he heads for the counter.

75A EXT. A BIRCHWOOD FOREST - DAY   75A

CLOSE on a chainsaw as it cuts through the trunk of a birch tree. PULL BACK to reveal a WORKER cutting down trees, several of which lie on the ground around him. Most of the forest has already been cleared.

OTTO (V.O.)
There used to be a forest up on
that hill. Birches, mostly.
(MORE)

72.

>   OTTO (V.O.) (CONT'D)
>   That's why they call it Birchwood.
>   But then they started building
>   condos, and they cut down all of
>   the birches...

75B   INT. PASTRY SHOP AND CAFE - DAY   75B

LATER: the pastries are gone. Otto and Marisol continue talking.

>   OTTO
>   ... They didn't even realize what
>   they'd done until Reuben and I told
>   them.
>
>   MARISOL
>   This was before the coup?
>
>   OTTO
>   (Nods:)
>   We were friends back then. But
>   after that, all we could see were
>   our differences -

INTERCUT (CAR SHOW MONTAGE/MEMORY) - In rapid succession:

- 1980s: Young Reuben backs a new FORD COUNTRY SQUIRE STATION WAGON out of his garage; Young Otto looks on disapprovingly;

- Young Otto backs a new CHEVY CAPRICE CLASSIC STATION WAGON out of his garage as Young Reuben looks on disapprovingly;

- 1990s: *REUBEN* backs a new FORD TAURUS STATION WAGON out of his garage, his son CHRIS (13) in the car as well. *OTTO* watches disapprovingly.

- Otto backs a new CHEVY SEDAN out of his garage. Reuben watches disapprovingly.

                                        END CAR SHOW MONTAGE.

76   INT. CAFE - DAY   76

Otto continues the story.

>   OTTO
>   Years later, I heard Reuben's son
>   Chris took a job in Japan. I don't
>   think he's visited since. He and
>   Reuben never did get along...

                                        FLASH BACK TO:

| 77 | EXT. OTTO'S STREET/REUBEN'S GARAGE, 1995 (MEMORY) - DAY | 77 |

Otto leaves his house with a bottle of high-end whisky.

> OTTO (V.O.)
> Anyway, that's when I decided it was time to bury the hatchet.

Otto sees Reuben walking down the road toward his garage.

> OTTO
> Reuben! Hey -

Otto hurries over to Reuben, pauses a moment before speaking.

> OTTO (CONT'D)
> Sonya gave me this a while back. Never found the occasion. And I thought maybe we could start fresh.

Otto holds out the bottle. Reuben gazes at it. A beat. He nods, takes the whisky.

> REUBEN
> We're friends, Otto. Always have been.
>   (He grins.)
> Hey, you want to see my new car?

> OTTO
> ... Sure.

Reuben goes over and raises his garage door, revealing a bright red convertible. He climbs in.

> REUBEN
> It's a new model. Just came out.

Otto stares in shock at the logo on the car's hood.

> OTTO
> ... Toyota? You bought a Toyota??

> REUBEN
>   (He nods, starts the car.)
> Celica GT convertible. 5-speed. Automatic.
>   (A little shrug:)
> You gotta change with the times.

Otto winces. As Reuben pulls the car out, Otto turns and starts walking away. Reuben calls after him.

                    REUBEN (CONT'D)
          Some people aren't very comfortable
          with change.

                                        END FLASHBACK.

78   INT. CAFÉ, 2018 - DAY   78

      Otto sits with Marisol, still smarting from the blow.

                    OTTO
          Automatic. I don't know what
          happened to Reuben - but that's
          when I knew I'd lost him. A man has
          to stand up for what he believes in
          - even if it's a goddamn Ford.

      A beat. Marisol tries to gently change the subject.

                    MARISOL
          Did you and Sonya ever think about
          having children?

      Otto looks up. Silence. He checks his watch, rises.

                    OTTO
          It's two o'clock.

79   EXT. OTTO'S GARAGE - DAY   79

      Otto and Marisol come out of his garage. He shuts the door.

                    MARISOL
          I was wondering if maybe you could
          help us out tonight. Tommy and I
          won't get many more chances to go
          out to dinner before the baby comes
          -

                    OTTO
          I'm not driving the two of you
          around on a date.

                    MARISOL
          Of course not. We'll get a cab.

                    OTTO
          What do you need me for, then?

80 INT. MARISOL AND TOMMY'S HOUSE - EVENING 80

Otto stands in the front hall, watching with growing impatience as Tommy taps buttons on his alarm system.

> TOMMY
> The alarm code is 4419. I'm setting it to 'Armed Stay' while we're gone. If you want to go out, you have to press this button to disarm it -

> OTTO
> I'm going to be here.

> TOMMY
> Right, but... Okay. Right.

Marisol enters, pulling on her coat. To Tommy:

> MARISOL
> Ready to go?

> OTTO
> I'm not sure this is a good idea.

> MARISOL
> Don't be silly. Just make sure the *pajarito* is in bed by nine -

> OTTO
> *Pajarito?*

> MARISOL
> 'Little bird' - Abbie. She won't want to go to sleep; sometimes telling her a story helps.
>   (She calls upstairs:)
> Bye, girls! Be good for *Abuelo* Otto!

> LUNA & ABBIE (O.S.)
> Yes, Mama! / We will!

Marisol and Tommy leave. Beat. Otto gazes anxiously upstairs.

81 INT. MARISOL AND TOMMY'S LIVING ROOM - EVENING 81

Luna is on the floor playing with her wrestling dolls; Abbie and Otto sit on the couch looking through a picture book called "Lucha Libre," which teaches Spanish and English words using wrestling images. Abbie is teaching Otto Spanish.

                    ABBIE
          "Eyes."

                    OTTO
               (Pronouncing the J sound:)
          "Ojos."

                    ABBIE
               (Laughs, corrects him:)
          "Oy-yos."

                    OTTO
          "Oy-yos."

                    ABBIE
          Good... *"Mouth."*

                    OTTO
          "Bah-ca."

                    ABBIE
               (Laughing:)
          "Bah-ca" means *"cow."* Try again:
          "B<u>oh</u>-ca."

                    OTTO
               (Straight-faced:)
          "Bah-ca."

                    ABBIE
          "B<u>oh</u>-ca."

                    OTTO
          "Bah-ca."

                    ABBIE
          Stop saying *"cow!"*

                                                  CUT TO:

Luna and Otto, each with one of Luna's wrestling dolls,
square off against each other. Otto pauses, shakes his head.

                    OTTO
          I don't think we should do this.

                    LUNA
          Why?

                    OTTO
          Because you don't stand a chance
          against *Luchadoro*.

                    LUNA
          Abuelo Luchadoro. Yaah!

Luna's doll leaps onto Otto's, pinning it to the ground.
Otto's doll flails, beats its plastic hand on the floor.

                    OTTO
          No, please! I surrender! Ahhh!

                                        CUT TO:

As Abbie and Luna play with the wrestling dolls, Otto rises,
noticing two diplomas hanging above a desk in the corner.

Both were awarded to Marisol Mendes. One is an undergraduate
degree in *Literatura* from the *Universidad de los Andes*. The
other is from UCLA - an M.A. in Latin American studies.

82   INT. MARISOL AND TOMMY'S KITCHEN - EVENING   82

Luna leads Otto into the kitchen and opens the fridge. Otto
carries Abbie in his arms. She looks sleepy and he looks
slightly out of his depth. Otto looks in the fridge.

                    OTTO
          There's no chocolate milk in here.

Luna takes out the milk and a bottle of chocolate syrup.

                    LUNA
          You make it with the syrup - but
          not too much, it'll keep her awake.

Otto notices an uninstalled dishwasher in the corner.

                    OTTO
          What's that?

                    LUNA
          That's the goddamn useless
          dishwasher. Dad said he wanted to
          throw it out the window, but Mom
          said Dad isn't allowed to open
          windows anymore.

83   I/E. LUNA AND ABBIE'S BEDROOM - NIGHT   83

Otto looks on as Luna builds a house in a computer program.
Abbie sits next to Luna, drinking chocolate milk.

                    OTTO
          You designed all of this?

LUNA
Mmm-hmm. I'm making the whole
neighborhood look the way I want...

Otto takes this in, nods in approval.

84 INT. MARISOL AND TOMMY'S HOUSE, FRONT HALL - NIGHT 84

Marisol and Tommy enter the house, one hobbling in on
crutches, the other very pregnant - both exhausted but happy.
Tommy turns off the alarm system.

MARISOL
Is your leg tired?

TOMMY
It's fine. Next week we go dancing.

MARISOL
It's a date.

Tommy glances upstairs.

TOMMY
It's awfully quiet.

They start up the steps.

85 INT. LUNA AND ABBIE'S BEDROOM - NIGHT 85

Marisol and Tommy enter the bedroom, surprised and pleased to
find Otto and Luna still sitting at the computer, with Abbie
in Otto's lap.

OTTO
She's already asleep.

Marisol takes Abbie from Otto's arms and carries her to bed.
Luna rises, picking up a small toy plastic hand on a stick.

LUNA
You did a good job tonight, Otto.
You should pat yourself on the
back.

She pats herself on the back with the little hand to
demonstrate, then holds it out to Otto. He considers, takes
it, pats himself on the back.

| 85A | INT. MARISOL AND TOMMY'S HOUSE, FRONT HALL - NIGHT | 85A |

Tommy looks out the front door, waving.

> TOMMY
> Thanks again, Otto. Good night.

He closes the door, sets the alarm.

| 85B | INT. MARISOL AND TOMMY'S KITCHEN - NIGHT | 85B |

Tommy goes into the kitchen. He is about to get a glass out of the cupboard when he notices that the dishwasher has been installed. Marisol enters. Tommy points to the dishwasher.

> TOMMY
> Did you know about this?

> MARISOL
> (Pleased:)
> Not at all.

| 86 | INT. OTTO'S BEDROOM - NIGHT | 86 |

Otto lies in bed, staring at the ceiling. He looks over at the Cat, which lies on the other pillow. Otto reaches out and runs a finger over the Cat's fur. The Cat purrs contentedly.

| 87 | EXT. OTTO'S STREET - DAY | 87 |

Morning. Otto is out on his rounds. He nears the gate, stops.

> OTTO
> Son of a...

BIRCHWOOD GROUNDSKEEPERS have parked work vehicles in front of the house near the gate. Where the Agent drove on the grass, the workers are rolling out artificial turf.

| 88 | EXT. OTTO'S NEIGHBORHOOD, RECYCLING AREA - DAY | 88 |

Otto mutters to himself as he sorts cans and bottles.

> OTTO
> Corporate blockhead... Why not add
> a windmill and a water hazard?

Malcolm appears, crosses to the nearby bike stand.

MALCOLM
Hi Otto.

Malcolm retrieves the bike from the stand and starts riding off. Otto hears something and waves for Malcolm to stop.

OTTO
Don't you hear that rattling sound your chain makes when you shift?

MALCOLM
Yeah, my bike's getting old.

OTTO
Don't blame the bike. You need to adjust your derailleur.

MALCOLM
My what?

88A EXT. OTTO'S STREET - DAY   88A

Jimmy is power-walking along the street. A car pulls up alongside him. SHARI KENZIE (20s) rolls down her window.

SHARI
Excuse me. My name is Shari Kenzie. I'm a social media journalist. I'm trying to find Otto Andersen.

JIMMY
Are you sure you want to do that?
(Pointing:)
I think he's at his garage - just around the corner down there.

89 I/E. OTTO'S GARAGE - DAY   89

Otto holds the bike while Malcolm adjusts the derailleur with a screwdriver. Malcolm spins the pedals. Silence.

MALCOLM
Wow. That's great. That's amazing.

OTTO
You treat it right, it will treat you right. Here - take this.

He puts the screwdriver in a tool pouch, hands it to Malcolm.

MALCOLM
Thanks, Otto. Really.

Malcolm climbs on, pedals up the street. Otto follows.

                    OTTO
          Can't believe I'm helping you throw
          crap on people's lawns. Isn't
          working two jobs enough?

                    MALCOLM
          I'm saving up for a car.

                    OTTO
              (Impressed:)
          Really? What kind?

                    MALCOLM
          A Volkswagen!

Otto takes this in, deeply pained, but says nothing.

A car pulls up near Otto and parks. Otto marches toward the car, waving for the driver to move on.

                    OTTO
          Hey, you're blocking that garage.

SHARI KENZIE (20s) climbs out of the car, smiling. She pulls out a card, pressing it into Otto's hand.

                    SHARI
          Mr. Anderson? My name is Shari
          Kenzie. I'm a social media
          journalist and -

                    OTTO
          A what?

                    SHARI
          I have an online series called
          "Everyday Heroes." What you did the
          other day at the train station was
          amazing. You saved that man's life!

Otto stiffens, turns and walks back towards his garage.

                    OTTO
          You've got the wrong person.

                    SHARI
          No, I don't. I've watched the video
          at least a dozen times. It's you.

                    OTTO
          What video?

Shari takes out her phone, pulls up the video as she speaks.

                    SHARI
          You haven't seen it? A commuter
          recorded what happened on their
          phone and posted it online. Someone
          in the comments section recognized
          you. That's how I tracked you down.
               (Pointing to the phone:)
          It's gotten over a million views.

                    OTTO
          A *million* - ?? Why can't people
          mind their own business?

Otto walks into the open garage. Shari follows him in.

                    SHARI
          Because stories like yours are
          inspiring. If I could just talk to
          you for a few minutes -

                    OTTO
          No, I don't have time for this.
          I've got things to do.

Otto slips past her, going back outside the garage.

                    SHARI
          I recorded a video message from the
          man you saved. You should see this.

                    MARISOL (O.S.)
          Good morning!

Otto sees Marisol approaching and panics - he closes the garage door with Shari inside and starts to walk away.

                    MARISOL (CONT'D)
          Ready for another driving lesson?

                    OTTO
          Not now.

Shari begins banging on the garage door from inside.

                    MARISOL
          What's going on in there?

                    OTTO
          Nothing - come on.

                    SHARI (O.S.)
          Hey! I'm still in here!

                    OTTO
          I didn't lock you in. Have you
          never opened a garage door? You
          turn the handle, for God's sake.
               (Walks away, muttering:)
          Idiots.

Shari opens the door. She and Marisol watch as Otto skulks off toward the house.

90   I/E. OTTO'S FRONT DOOR - DAY   90

Marisol knocks on Otto's door. Knocks again.

                    MARISOL
          Otto, it's me... She's gone now.

Otto opens his door, sullenly pulling his coat back on.

                    OTTO
          Good. I still haven't finished my
          morning rounds.

He comes outside and heads toward the gates. Marisol follows.

                    OTTO (CONT'D)
          Social media journalist - what the
          hell does that even mean? It's all
          just a bunch of fools pointing
          cameras at themselves.

                    MARISOL
          You handled that well, closing her
          up in your garage. Good job.

Marisol laughs. Otto tries to remain sullen, but gradually begins to "almost smile." Marisol laughs harder. Otto gives her a playful shove. They walk together, enjoying the moment.

                    MARISOL (CONT'D)
          I've been thinking -

                    OTTO
          Don't brag.

                    MARISOL
          Seriously - you've done so much for
          us. I want to do something for you.

                    OTTO
          I don't need anything.

MARISOL
You could do with some decent food sometimes.

OTTO
(Shrugs.)
Those *salpors* weren't bad.

MARISOL
And I could help you clean out that front hall, pack up some of those old coats and shoes of Sonya's so you're not always looking at them.

OTTO
(Tensing:)
There's no need.

MARISOL
No, but it might help you move on.

OTTO
I don't want to move on.

MARISOL
I'm not saying you should forget her, Otto - she'll always be with you. But you're still here and -

OTTO
Enough.

MARISOL
When my father died, my mother stopped living. She spent the rest of her life in mourning -

OTTO
(Finally erupting:)
Stop talking!

MARISOL
Don't yell at me!

OTTO
... Why can't people mind their own business? Idiots, interrupting me at every turn. The more they babble on, the more they drown out the memory of her voice. I don't want to clear Sonya out of my life. She was everything. There was nothing before her; there's nothing after.

                    MARISOL
            (Unexpectedly hurt.)
    I'm something.

Beat. Just then, the Dye & Merica Agent, whose car was parked down by Reuben and Anita's house, drives past. At the end of the street near the garages, he turns the car around the center meridian and heads back toward the gates.

                    OTTO
    You son of a BITCH!

Otto sees where the car is headed and runs to cut it off, planting himself directly in the car's path.

                    OTTO (CONT'D)
    Back up! Now!

The Agent stops, gets out. Marisol watches at a distance as the Agent approaches Otto.

                    DYE & MERICA AGENT
    What are you doing, Otto? You're
    not helping Reuben and Anita by
    doing this - I hope you know that.

                    OTTO
    I don't give a damn about them. I
    do give a damn about people
    following the rules.

The Agent steps close to Otto, patient concern in his tone.

                    DYE & MERICA AGENT
    Yes, I know. I know all about you,
    Otto. They have a file on you in
    the office that's this thick.
            (Holding fingers apart:)
    I know about your wife, how you
    blame what happened to her on
    everyone else -

                    OTTO
    Shut up! One more word, I swear -

Otto flinches, chest tightening. The Agent raises his hands.

                    DYE & MERICA AGENT
    Otto, take it easy. I'm really not
    trying to upset you -
            (Lowering his voice:)
    You see, I work in the Healthcare
    and Assisted Living division of my
    company;
                    (MORE)

>   DYE & MERICA AGENT (CONT'D)
>   we know a lot more about you than
>   you probably realize.
>   (Points to Otto's chest:)
>   Look after that heart of yours.

The Agent turns and walks back to his car. Otto follows.

>   OTTO
>   What do you know about my heart?

The Agent gets in, shuts the door. Otto bangs on the window.

>   OTTO (CONT'D)
>   What do you know about my heart?
>   Huh? What do you know?!

The Agent turns the car and drives off toward the entrance gate. Otto keeps up with the car, banging on the window.

>   OTTO (CONT'D)
>   Stop the car!! You prying bastard!!

Otto flinches, falls behind. Marisol sees this, frightened.

>   MARISOL
>   Are you okay? Otto, what's - ?

>   OTTO
>   Just leave me alone!!

He storms off toward his house.

91   I/E. OTTO'S HOUSE, HALLWAY/FRONT DOOR - DAY   91

Otto bursts into his house in a rage. He slams his door.

>   MARISOL (O.S.)
>   (Outside:)
>   Goddamn it, Otto! Talk to me!

Otto locks the door. He paces, pounds his fists into the coats that hang in the hall, then buries his face in them.

92   I/E. OTTO'S LIVING ROOM - DAY   92

Otto sits on the couch. Marisol pounds on the door, then walks over to look through the window, trying to get Otto's attention.

>   MARISOL
>   Otto, please - just let me in!

OUTSIDE, Marisol finally gives up, walking away from the door in defeat.

INSIDE, Otto, still on the couch, FLASHES ON A BRIEF MEMORY: *Young Otto* pounds nails into wood, cuts scrollwork into a small headboard...

END MEMORY.

93 INT. OTTO'S ATTIC - DAY (NIAGARA MEMORIES SEQUENCE) 93

Otto (60s) climbs up the stairs into the attic. The only light comes from one window. Otto has covered the attic vents with clear plastic sheeting for the winter.

Otto sees a little rocking crib in the corner covered with plastic sheeting, its headboard decorated with simple scrollwork.

- MEMORY: *Young Otto* sets the crib up in the BEDROOM as a very pregnant Sonya looks on, delighted.

END MEMORY.

BACK IN THE ATTIC, Otto (60s) finds a camping lantern which he lights and sets atop an old dresser next to a tattered cap that says "Niagara Falls" on it.

- MEMORY: Sonya, pregnant, wears the Niagara cap as she and *Young Otto* sit down to breakfast. Otto sets a camera on the table. They are poolside, spending their first morning in a NIAGARA FALLS HOTEL.

  A Waiter pours them coffee, sets a bear-shaped honey dispenser on the table which Sonya has asked for. She squeezes a little honey into her coffee, stirs it, then lifts the cup, toasts Otto. Young Otto toasts her back.

- ANOTHER MEMORY: Sonya and Young Otto ride the *Maid of the Mist* ferry. Otto takes pictures of Sonya. As they pass under the falls, Sonya pulls Young Otto into a kiss.

- ANOTHER MEMORY: The cap rests in Sonya's lap. Otto wears his camera on a strap around his neck. She and Young Otto are in a BUS that drives along a scenic WINDING ROAD.

            SONYA
    Give me your hand.

Otto does so. Sonya presses his hand to her belly.

            SONYA (CONT'D)
    The baby's really kicking.

Young Otto nods, smiling.

                                              END MEMORY.

BACK IN THE ATTIC: *Otto (60s)* finds Lucas's shotgun case. He opens it, revealing the barrel, finds bullets. He glances to the attic vent, pulls down the plastic sheeting.

94   INT. OTTO'S DINING ROOM - DAY   94

Otto moves the dining table and chairs to the corner of the room. He uses plastic sheeting to cover one wall and partially seal off the room, and he covers the floor with a drop cloth.

95   INT. OTTO'S BEDROOM - SUNSET   95

Otto pulls a dress shirt on over his tee shirt and boxers. His best suit lies on the bed. As Otto buttons the shirt, he glances in the mirror, pauses. He takes the shirt back off, hanging it along with his suit back in the closet.

Otto notices the Cat watching him. He gets an emergency radio out of his dresser, cranks it up for power, tunes it to classical music, then sets it on the bed stand near the Cat.

96   INT. OTTO'S DINING ROOM - DUSK   96

The sun has just set outside the half-closed blinds. Otto sits in his underwear on a dining chair, desolate, the shotgun case and lantern at his feet. Classical music plays upstairs, continuing under the scene as Otto remembers...

97   INT. BUS (MEMORY) - DAY   97

As before, Sonya puts Young Otto's hand on her belly. We don't hear her as she asks Otto if he feels the baby moving.

Young Otto nods and smiles. He excuses himself and goes up the aisle to the restroom at the back of the bus.

98   I/E. BUS/BUS BATHROOM (MEMORY) - DAY   98

Young Otto closes the door to the BUS BATHROOM. He takes the camera strap from around his neck, sets the camera on the sink, then gets a tissue to wipe away tears of happiness.

BACK IN HER SEAT, Sonya gazes serenely out the window at the passing landscape.

In the BATHROOM, Otto finishes washing his hands. He looks up, smiling at his reflection in the mirror.

REVERSE ANGLE - revealing *Otto (60s)* gazing at himself, living out this moment as he has done every day since.

And then the bus SHAKES, THROWING Otto side-to-side as it CRASHES. Debris flies through the air as the bus ROLLS OVER and the bathroom walls themselves are ripped apart.

Light floods in and the scene FADES TO WHITE, BLURRING...

99 EXT. CRASH SITE (MEMORY) - DAY   99

Young Otto climbs out of the wreckage, bruised and disheveled. He looks around, dazed.

INJURED PASSENGERS are everywhere, some unconscious, some weeping, some tending to others. The bus is on its side thirty or so yards away, ripped open and partially crushed.

Young Otto rises and stumbles toward the wreckage.

He finds his camera among the debris. Then he finds the torn Niagara Falls cap.

100 INT. OTTO'S DINING ROOM (MODERN DAY) - DUSK/INTERCUT   100

Otto opens the shotgun case, takes out the shotgun.

101 INT. HOSPITAL, HALLWAY (MEMORY) - DAY   101

Young Otto stands in the hallway of a hospital, clutching the tattered cap. A doctor (DR. KNIGHT) and a social worker (ANNA) come out to speak to him.

                  DR. KNIGHT
Mr. Anderson? I'm very sorry - I have some bad news. Your wife is still unconscious; she's sustained a serious spinal injury. I'm afraid the baby didn't make it. This is Anna - she's going to talk to you. Again, I'm very sorry.

                  ANNA
Let's have a seat, Mr. Anderson.

Young Otto is in a daze. She guides him to a chair.

> ANNA (CONT'D)
> I know this is a very difficult
> time for you. Do you have any
> family or friends you would like us
> to call?

102 INT. OTTO'S LIVING ROOM (MODERN DAY) - DUSK/INTERCUT 102

Otto loads the shotgun.

103 INT. HOSPITAL ROOM/BATHROOM (MEMORY) - DAY/EVENING 103

Young Otto sits by Sonya's bedside. She lies unconscious, face and arms covered in scrapes and bandages.

ANOTHER DAY - Young Otto dozes by Sonya's bed, wearing fresh clothes. Sonya's bandages are gone. She's still unconscious.

IN THE BATHROOM of the hospital room, Young Otto uses an electric shaver to trim his stubble, regards *Otto (60s)*, the older version of himself in the mirror.

Young Otto comes out of the bathroom, then stops, watching as Sonya, eyes still closed, holds her hand out, extending her index finger. Young Otto takes her finger in his palm.

Sonya opens her eyes and looks around, still foggy. She sees Young Otto, starts to smile, then hesitates, apprehensive.

CUT TO:

EVENING - Young Otto holds Sonya; she weeps, unconsolable.

104 INT. OTTO'S DINING ROOM (MODERN DAY) - NIGHT 104

Otto puts the butt of the shotgun on the floor and presses the barrel to his forehead.

The MUSIC UPSTAIRS STOPS PLAYING.

Otto reconsiders, puts the barrel in his mouth, then draws back at the taste. He rests his chin on the barrel, closes his eyes and puts his finger on the trigger.

> SONYA (V.O.)
> That's enough now, darling...

Otto opens his eyes as he remembers:

Sonya's face, smiling, tears in her eyes. They are sitting together at the dining table. Sonya is in a wheelchair. She reaches out to touch Otto's cheek.

> SONYA
> You're angry, I know. And sad - so am I. But now we have to live.

END MEMORY.

Otto's finger relaxes on the trigger.

The Cat slips into the room and sits facing Otto, watching him. Beat. Otto moves the shotgun out from under his chin.

Someone knocks at the door, startling Otto. He flinches, blasting a shotgun round into the ceiling. Plaster rains down. The Cat scrambles out of the room, terrified.

105 I/E. OTTO'S HALLWAY, FRONT DOOR - NIGHT 105

Otto throws open the door, still in his underwear, shotgun and camping lantern in hand.

> OTTO
> What?!

Malcolm, outside, reels backward, staring at the shotgun.

> MALCOLM
> I'm sorry! I didn't mean to -

> OTTO
> Oh, for God's sake - I'm not going to shoot you!

> MALCOLM
> What was that noise?

> OTTO
> ... Generator must have blown. Power's out. What do you want?
>   (Beat.)
> What? Come on, it's freezing.

> MALCOLM
> ... I was hoping you might let me crash on your couch for the night.

> OTTO
> This isn't a hotel.

MALCOLM
(He starts to leave.)
No. I'm sorry -

OTTO
Why can't you go home?

MALCOLM
My dad kicked me out.

106   INT. OTTO'S FRONT HALL/ STAIRS/ UPSTAIRS HALL - NIGHT   106

Otto leads Malcolm into the house, heads for the staircase. Malcolm follows.

OTTO
Don't go in the dining room.
Ceiling needs fixing.
(He gestures upstairs:)
There's a couch in Sonya's old
study you can use.

MALCOLM
Great. Thanks for this.

As they head upstairs:

OTTO
Why'd he throw you out? Because
you're Malcolm now?

MALCOLM
(Shrugs, wryly:)
Because I'm Malcolm, because I
dress like this, I read too much, I
don't like sports - take your pick.
I'm not what he wanted in a son.

OTTO
(Meaning it:)
Then he's an idiot.

They've reached the top of the stairs. Otto hands Malcolm the lantern, gestures to Sonya's study.

OTTO (CONT'D)
You're in there.

MALCOLM
Okay. 'Night.

Otto grunts. Malcolm goes into Sonya's study. Otto heads back downstairs.

106AA INT. OTTO'S DINING ROOM - NIGHT   106AA

Otto returns to the dining room, glancing from the hole in the ceiling to the bits of plaster that have rained down onto the floor. He goes into the kitchen, then returns with a dustpan and whisk broom and begins cleaning up the mess.

106A   EXT. OTTO'S HOUSE - MORNING   106A

Establishing.

107   INT. OTTO'S BEDROOM - MORNING   107

Morning. Otto's eyes open.

108   INT. OTTO'S HALLWAY/KITCHEN/DINING ROOM - MORNING   108

Otto comes downstairs and heads for the kitchen. He stops in the doorway, surprised. Malcolm is already feeding the Cat. Malcolm sees Otto and rises, crossing to a pan on the stove.

> MALCOLM
> Good morning! The power's still out, so I figured I'd cook up the last of the eggs while they're still good. I hope you don't mind.

Otto looks around uncomfortably, turns to go.

> OTTO
> I have to do my morning rounds.

> MALCOLM
> Don't you at least want some coffee first?

Beat. Otto looks at his watch, nods.

Malcolm gets out coffee cups. Otto crosses into the Dining Room, which he cleaned up after Malcolm went to bed. The dining table and chairs are back where they belong and the ceiling has been patched with duct tape.

Malcolm enters with two coffee cups and sits, handing one of the cups to Otto and raising the other cup in a toast.

Otto struggles with how to respond. He finally lowers his eyes and takes a sip. Beat. Nods in approval.

LATER - Malcolm talks as Otto savors an omelet.

MALCOLM (CONT'D)
When I told him I was thinking of getting a car, he said I needed to start paying him room and board first. It got worse from there.

OTTO
(Shaking his head. Beat.)
You didn't tell him you were looking at a Volkswagen, did you?

MALCOLM
No.

OTTO
Then there's no excuse.
(Checks his watch, rises.)
I really have to get to my rounds.

MALCOLM
Can I tag along?

OTTO
... It's a free country.

109 EXT. OTTO'S STREET/GATE/RECYCLING AREA - DAY 109

Otto and Malcolm walk down the street on their rounds.

- In the RECYCLING AREA, they work together to sort the bins. As they come out of the Recycling Area, Jimmy power-walks up to them.

JIMMY
Hey Otto, mind if I join you? I need to get my steps in.

Otto gives a half-shrug *("Whatever")*, continues walking. Jimmy falls in alongside him, waving to Malcolm.

JIMMY (CONT'D)
I'm Jimmy.

MALCOLM
Malcolm. Nice to meet you.

- They walk back up the block, checking parking permits as they go. Malcolm checks permits on the other side of the street.

MALCOLM (CONT'D)
Yes... yes... yes...

- They reach the GATE. Otto tugs on it to be sure it's latched. Malcolm and Jimmy each tug on the gate as well.

As they walk back past Anita and Reuben's house, Jimmy notices Reuben sitting in the window. He turns to Otto.

> JIMMY
> Otto, did you hear they're coming to move Reuben into assisted living this afternoon?

> OTTO
> Who is?

> JIMMY
> The Dye & Merica guys.

> OTTO
> (Sighs, keeps walking.)
> My God. So they convinced Anita to sell them the house?

> JIMMY
> No. They made the deal with Chris.

> OTTO
> Chris? He can't do that.

> JIMMY
> Yeah, he can. After Dye & Merica found out Anita had Parkinson's, they tracked Chris down -

> OTTO
> (This stops him.)
> Parkinson's?

> JIMMY
> Yeah, last year Chris convinced Anita to give him power of attorney in case she got worse. So Dye & Merica made the deal with Chris to buy the house.

> OTTO
> (Overwhelmed:)
> Those pricks -
> (Back to Jimmy:)
> Wait - Anita found out she had Parkinson's *last year?* That's not right - she would have told Sonya. And Sonya would have told me.

JIMMY
Anita and Reuben didn't want you
and Sonya to know. They said you
had enough on your plate as it is.

OTTO
(This hits him hard.)
... They said that?

110 I/E. ANITA AND REUBEN'S HOUSE - DAY   110

Anita answers her front door. Otto stands outside.

OTTO
I need to see everything you've
ever gotten from Dye & Merica -
letters, notices. Do you have a
copy of the power of attorney?

ANITA
(Surprised:)
How do you know - ?

OTTO
Do you have it?

ANITA
Yes.

Otto moves past her into the house.

OTTO
Get it. And any records you have
about Reuben's condition and yours.

ANITA
Did Jimmy tell you - ?

OTTO
Now!

Anita hurries into the back of the house. Otto sees Reuben
sitting by the window, goes to him. Pause.

OTTO (CONT'D)
I've been an idiot. I got so
wrapped up in my own troubles, I
wasn't thinking about anyone else.
I figured they weren't thinking
about me. But. Friends shouldn't do
that. So.
(Pause.)
(MORE)

                    OTTO (CONT'D)
          It isn't easy to say after all this
          time, but I'm sorry. And I'll get
          this sorted out.

Reuben slowly extends the fingers of his right hand toward
Otto. Otto realizes what Reuben is trying to do; he takes
Reuben's hand and shakes it.

111   I/E. MARISOL AND TOMMY'S HOUSE, FRONT DOOR - DAY   111

Otto knocks on the front door, arms loaded with paper and
files. Marisol answers, regards Otto coolly.

                    OTTO
          I need to use your phone.

                    MARISOL
          Can't you use your own?

                    OTTO
          It's disconnected. At the moment.

                    MARISOL
          Why, for God's sake?

                    OTTO
          It doesn't matter. I just need to
          use your phone, okay?

                    MARISOL
          ... You know what? No.

                    OTTO
          No?

                    MARISOL
          No. You won't tell me why your
          phone is disconnected, you won't
          tell me why you need to use the
          phone, you wouldn't tell me what
          happened to you out in the street
          yesterday, and then you went inside
          and wouldn't even answer the door -
              (Growing emotional,
               despite herself:)
          You scared me, Otto. Do you know
          how long I was out there? I didn't
          know if something happened to you
          or if something was going to happen
          - and I'm sorry if I said the wrong
          thing about Sonya's old coats but I
          was just trying to help and _you
          left me out there_...
                    (MORE)

98.

> MARISOL (CONT'D)
> So no, you can't use the phone...
> (She starts to close the
> door, opens it again.)
> You think your life is so hard and everyone is an idiot so you have to do it all on your own - well, guess what? You can't. No one can. And you should be happy that someone actually wanted to help you get through a crap day - even if they are an idiot. So...

Beat. She starts to close the door again.

> OTTO
> The real estate bastards are trying to force Reuben and Anita out of their home. That's why I need to use your phone.

> MARISOL
> (Shakes her head, sighs.)
> I'll get my cellphone.

She leaves the door open, walks back inside.

112 INT. MARISOL AND TOMMY'S HOUSE, DINING ROOM/KITCHEN - DAY 112

Marisol crosses into the dining room, still upset. Otto appears in the doorway behind her, paperwork in his arms.

Marisol gets her cellphone from the dining room table and holds it out to Otto. He sets the paperwork down, takes the phone. Marisol crosses into the kitchen to wait while Otto makes his call. Otto watches her through the doorway. Pause.

> OTTO
> We'd never had a vacation. Sonya was six months pregnant and wanted to do something special before the baby came, so we booked a trip to Niagara Falls. On the way back home, the bus crashed. There was a recall on the brake lines; the company never got them fixed. Sonya was paralyzed. And we lost our son.

Marisol crosses to the dining table, sinks into one of the chairs.

113 EXT. OTTO AND SONYA'S HOUSE, 1981 (MEMORY) - DAY 113

A grim *Young Otto* lifts a smiling Sonya out of the passenger seat of their station wagon and sets her in her wheelchair.

> OTTO (V.O.)
> It was three months before she was finally able to come home.

As Young Otto wheels Sonya up the metal ramp that leads to the front door of the house, he glances over at all the new construction that's begun on the far end of the street.

> OTTO (V.O.)
> By then, they had started building new condos, community centers and walkways - none of which were designed for wheelchair access.

114 INT. COMMUNITY CENTER, 1982 (MEMORY) - DAY 114

Young Otto carries Sonya through the narrow doorway of a community center. Young Reuben guides her folded wheelchair through the door and opens it for her. Young Anita helps her sit.

A handful of people have already arrived in the room. A banner up front reads: "BIRCHWOOD HOMEOWNER'S ASSOCIATION."

> OTTO (V.O.)
> Of course, the builders could have changed the plans, but the laws weren't in place back then and they didn't give a shit. I did -

LATER - the room is nearly full. Two DYE & MERICA REPS stand at the front; one of them talks about improvements they're planning for Birchwood while the other points at blueprints on a cork board.

> DYE & MERICA REP 1
> ... And we're also putting in a new playground and a daycare center -

Young Otto, sitting at the front, rises.

> YOUNG OTTO
> None of this is wheelchair accessible. And you still haven't fixed any of the doors in the old buildings or put in ramps -

                    DYE & MERICA REP 2
               We have to set priorities. Right
               now we're focused on the needs of
               young families with kids.

                    DYE & MERICA REP 1
               Birchwood living is not for
               everyone. But there are plenty of
               places these days for people like
               your wife -

                    YOUNG OTTO
                    (Growing irate:)
               What does that mean - people like
               her? What does that mean?!

     Young Otto explodes with anger, striding forward and shoving
     the man. The other rep and Young Reuben move to restrain him.

                    OTTO (V.O.)
               I'd fought them before, I'd fight
               them again. But I was so angry -

                                                  END MEMORY.

115 INT. MARISOL AND TOMMY'S HOUSE, LIVING ROOM - DAY   115

     Otto, now sitting beside Marisol, continues his story.

                    OTTO
               That's when I was voted out as head
               of the Homeowner's Association.
                    (Beat.)
               I wanted to obliterate them all -
               the builders, the realtors, the bus
               company, the bus driver. I would
               never have been able to move on
               without Sonya. She said we had to
               keep on living. So I did...

                                                  FLASH BACK TO:

115A INT. ANOTHER HOSPITAL ROOM, SIX MONTHS AGO - DAY   115A

     Otto sits beside another hospital bed. Sonya lies in bed,
     slightly turned away from him, her face hidden. Otto holds
     Sonya's hand in his, clasping her index finger with his other
     hand.

                    OTTO (V.O.)
               I lived for her.

Sonya's grip weakens; her hand goes slack.

                    OTTO (V.O.)
          Then six months ago she passed
          away. She had cancer.

                                        END FLASHBACK.

115B   INT. MARISOL AND TOMMY'S HOUSE, DINING ROOM - CONTINUOUS   115B

       Marisol places her hand on top of Otto's. He clasps it. Beat.

                    OTTO
          I was going to join her. That's why
          my phone is disconnected. But I
          think she wants me to keep living.

       Otto slips his hand free, rises. He lifts the cellphone,
       pulls out a business card.

                    OTTO (CONT'D)
          And I've got things to do.

116   EXT. OTTO'S STREET, GATE ENTRANCE - DAY   116

       The Dye & Merica Agent unlatches the gate, swings it open. A
       wheelchair transportation van with the Dye & Merica logo
       drives through the gate. The Agent goes to his car, follows.

117   EXT. ANITA AND REUBEN'S HOUSE - DAY   117

       The van and the car pull up to Anita's house. Otto sits on
       the stoop, the Cat in his lap. He taps on Anita's window.

       Two ELDERCARE TRANSPORT WORKERS get out of the van. The Agent
       gets out of his car, walks up the front path.

                    DYE & MERICA AGENT
          You're wasting your time, Otto.
          This is a done deal. Reuben is
          coming with us, and if you get in
          our way, I'll have you arrested.

       Otto raises his hands in mock surrender. Anita comes outside.

                    OTTO
          I'm not going to do a thing.

                    ANITA
          Don't take another step. You are
          not taking my husband away from me.

                    DYE & MERICA AGENT
                (A patronizing smile:)
            Anita, please - we're doing this
            for your own good.

                    ANITA
            No. You're doing this to get my
            property. I want Reuben to be able
            to spend his last years right here
            with me in our home.

                    DYE & MERICA AGENT
            And who's going to take care of
            Reuben when you're no longer able
            to do so? Hmm? Who's going to take
            care of you? Otto? He's not in the
            best health either - are you, Otto?

                    JIMMY (O.S.)
            I'll take care of them.

The Agent turns. Jimmy, Marisol and Tommy have all emerged
from Jimmy's house next door. They are all filming different
angles of the scene on their phones.

                    DYE & MERICA AGENT
            What are you doing? Put those down.

                    JIMMY
            Anita and Reuben are like family to
            me. I'll take care of them as long
            as they need.

                    DYE & MERICA AGENT
            Well, they're not your family - and
            their son Chris has decided they
            aren't fit to be on their own, so -

Shari Kenzie appears from behind the others. Malcolm films
her as she speaks using Shari's own high-end digital camera.

                    SHARI
            Excuse me - when was the last time
            Chris saw his parents? He lives in
            Japan - they've been estranged for
            ten years. Chris would have no idea
            how his parents are doing - except
            for what *you* told him.

The Agent tenses, his usual calm demeanor evaporating.

                    DYE & MERICA AGENT
            Okay - who are you?

                    SHARI
          My name is Shari Kenzie. We're
          streaming live right now.

                    DYE & MERICA AGENT
              (Goes ashen.)
          What? Turn those cameras off! You
          can't film this!

                    OTTO
          It's a public sidewalk.

                    SHARI
          You told Anita's son Chris that she
          had Parkinson's - but Anita never
          told anyone about her diagnosis. So
          how did you know?

                    DYE & MERICA AGENT
              (Faltering:)
          I would have to check the records -

                    SHARI
          Mr. Anderson over there is
          something of a local hero. He tells
          me you know details about his
          private health records as well.

The Agent turns, glaring, face turning red with anger. Otto
nods, the barest glint of victory in his eyes.

                    SHARI (CONT'D)
          So how are you and your company
          getting illegal access to the
          medical records of seniors?

The Agent waves the Transport Workers back toward their van.

                    DYE & MERICA AGENT
          Okay, let's go - we're done here.

The Agent heads to his car. Shari follows, playing to camera.

                    SHARI
          I first uploaded Anita and Reuben's
          story an hour ago; already dozens
          of people are saying Dye & Merica
          forced them out of their homes -

                    DYE & MERICA AGENT
          We're done! Get that goddamn camera
          away from me!

Otto watches from the porch as the Agent climbs into his car. He glances over, sees Reuben sitting in the front window.

118 INT. ANITA AND REUBEN'S HOUSE - DAY 118

Otto and Reuben sit by the window.

> OTTO
> He just rolled over, gave up. In our day, the bastards would have at least put up a fight, you know?
> (Beat.)
> It doesn't make up for all they put us through over the years - but they haven't gotten rid of us yet.

Reuben slowly smiles. Otto leans in, smiling as well.

> OTTO (CONT'D)
> Yeah, it does feel pretty good, doesn't it?

119 EXT. ANITA AND REUBEN'S HOUSE/STREET - DAY 119

Otto steps outside, picking up the Cat on the porch and tucking it under his arm. Anita and Jimmy are still being interviewed by Shari as Malcolm films them. Marisol and Tommy look on.

> JIMMY
> ... Oh, yeah - I have dinner at their house nearly every night.

> ANITA
> Jimmy does a lot of the shopping for me already...

Otto slips past them, trying to avoid notice. As he reaches the street, he slows - then staggers. He strains to set the cat down gently, then collapses, sprawling onto the pavement. Marisol sees him first and rushes to his side.

> MARISOL
> Otto! Otto!
> (To the others:)
> Call an ambulance!

> OTTO
> (Lifts his head, weakly:)
> Don't let them drive past the gate... You can drive me.

| 120 | OMITTED | 120 |

| 121 | INT. HOSPITAL HALLWAY - DAY | 121 |

Marisol waits anxiously in a hospital corridor. A NURSE approaches.

                  NURSE
Ms. Mendes? You can come in and see him now.

                  MARISOL
Good - yes, thank you -

| 121A | INT. OTTO'S HOSPITAL ROOM - DAY | 121A |

Marisol enters Otto's hospital room. Otto lies in bed, wearing an oxygen mask and hooked to monitors. Marisol goes to Otto's side, fighting emotion. He opens his eyes, places a hand on her cheek.

DR. ELLIS (female, 40s) enters, flipping through a chart.

                  DR. ELLIS
Marisol? I'm Doctor Ellis. Mr. Anderson listed you as next of kin.

                  MARISOL
Yes - correct -

                  DR. ELLIS
Your uncle had a close call. Has he spoken to you about his condition?

                  MARISOL
Not really, no.

                  DR. ELLIS
It's called Hypertrophic Cardiomyopathy. Basically, his heart is too big.

                  MARISOL
... *Too big?*

Marisol begins laughing. She tries to stop herself, then Otto opens his eyes and smiles - which makes her laugh harder. Dr. Ellis looks on, bemused.

                  MARISOL (CONT'D)
You're really bad at dying, you know that?

Marisol's laughter turns to shallow panting. She doubles over as she feels contractions coming on.

> MARISOL (CONT'D)
> *¡Ay - mierda!* I think it's time, Otto! *¡¡¡MIERDA!!!*

Marisol turns to Dr. Ellis for help.

> DR. ELLIS
> Oh - I'm a cardiologist. I'll send someone in for you.

Dr. Ellis leaves.

FADE TO:

122 EXT. MARISOL AND TOMMY'S HOUSE - DAY   122

Blue balloons fly outside Marisol and Tommy's house.

123 INT. MARISOL AND TOMMY'S HOUSE, LIVING ROOM - DAY   123

Inside, eight or so GUESTS - including a few family members, some of Tommy's co-workers, parents of other school kids and the kids themselves - have gathered along with Tommy, Marisol, Abbie and Luna to celebrate the arrival of the new baby.

Food has been set out for the guests. Marisol holds her son in her arms; others gather around, smiling and greeting the little one.

Otto enters from the front of the house.

> MARISOL
> Otto, hi! Everyone, this is my friend, Otto.

The guests all greet Otto with beaming smiles - clearly Marisol has already told everyone about him. Otto nods hello, the attention making him uncomfortable.

> OTTO
> (To Marisol:)
> Could you come with me for a minute?

> MARISOL
> (Following him:)
> Of course. Is this about all the cars parked out front?

                    OTTO
          No - I brought you something.

A large object bundled in a blanket sits in the ENTRY HALL.
Otto removes the blanket. It is the crib he made, complete
with a new mattress and fresh bedding.

                    MARISOL
               (Deeply moved:)
          Otto -

                    OTTO
          I gave it a fresh coat of paint.
          Non-toxic. It's for the baby.

                    MARISOL
          I love it. Thank you. It's perfect.
               (Handing Otto the baby:)
          Here, hold him for me - I want to
          show Tommy.

Marisol hurries off in search of Tommy. Otto down at the
baby. He smiles, emotional.

                    OTTO
          Hello there. *Hola.* I'm Otto.
          O-t-t-o... *Pajarito* - that's you
          now.

Otto places the baby in the crib, gently rocking it.

                    OTTO (CONT'D)
          See? It works. You like that? Good.

124   EXT. CEMETERY - DAY   124

Tree branches in springtime, lush and green.

TILT DOWN to discover Otto setting his thermos and lawn chair
down in front of Sonya's headstone. Marisol stands behind
Otto, the baby in her arms. Tommy, Luna, Abbie and the Cat
are there as well.

Otto gestures to each in turn, 'introducing' them to Sonya.
Marisol takes the baby's hand in hers and waves to Sonya.
Luna and Abbie place fresh pink flowers on the headstone.

TILT UP toward the barren trees that surround the cemetery.

                                             MATCH FADE TO:

| 125 | OMITTED | 125 |

| 126 | INT. OTTO'S BEDROOM - MORNING | 126 |

Otto dresses before the bedroom mirror, surprised to discover he has trouble buttoning the lower buttons of his shirt.

| 127 | INT. OTTO'S KITCHEN - MORNING | 127 |

Otto takes a *salpor* from a large plate of them on the kitchen table, washing a bite down with coffee, then scooping leftover chicken and rice into the colorful bowl.

As Otto bends to put the bowl on the floor, he winces, a chest pain coming on. He sits. The pain subsides. Otto finishes the *salpor*, thinking.

| 128 | INT. OTTO'S BEDROOM - MORNING | 128 |

Otto sits at Sonia's bedroom vanity writing a letter. Abbie's drawing of Otto is tucked into the frame of the mirror.

Otto puts the letter and a sheaf of documents into a large envelope, writes something on the outside of the envelope and tucks it upright behind the corner of the mirror.

| 129 | EXT. OTTO'S HOUSE - DAY | 129 |

Tommy carries a cardboard box out from Otto's house, placing it in the open trunk of Otto's car.

| 130 | INT. OTTO'S HOUSE, LIVING ROOM/ENTRY HALL - DAY | 130 |

In the LIVING ROOM, Otto has patched up the hole in his ceiling and now stands on a chair painting over it. Nearby, Luna and Abbie are playing with their baby brother, who is old enough now to sit upright.

In the ENTRY HALL, Marisol has nearly finished packing up Sonya's old coats. Otto enters, paintbrush still in hand, gazing at the empty wall hooks. Marisol notices. Otto looks at her, nods *(It's okay. Go ahead and finish)*.

| 131 | EXT. OTTO'S GARAGE - DAY | 131 |

Later. Otto, Malcolm and Jimmy watch as Otto shows them how to put oil in the Chevy Malibu. He has them finish the job and goes to get something out of the glove compartment.

Otto returns as they close the hood. He sets the car's registration on the hood, signs it and holds it out to Malcolm, along with keys. Malcolm and Jimmy are stunned. Malcolm fights emotion, draws Otto into an awkward hug.

| 132 | EXT. MARISOL AND TOMMY'S HOUSE - DAY | 132 |

A new Chevy Silverado pulls up in front, the driver honking the horn.

Marisol, Tommy and the children all come outside and gather around. Otto climbs out, proudly showing off his purchase.

> MARISOL
> Oh, my God. It's so big!

> OTTO
> I wanted to have enough room for everyone. Come on!

Tommy stands on the porch with the baby in his arms, watching as Marisol and the girls climb into the truck.

| 133 | I/E. CHEVY SILVERADO - DAY | 133 |

CLOSE ON Otto putting a booster seat into the back seat of the Silverado, which he has covered with newspaper. Marisol buckles Abbie into her seat on the other side of the car as Tommy watches on from the porch steps, holding the baby.

Otto helps Luna climb into the truck, then gets into the driver's seat, Marisol beside him in the front. He starts the engine, checks the rearview mirror, glances to Marisol and smiles.

> OTTO
> This is living.

| 134 | I/E. CHEVY SILVERADO/OPEN ROAD - DAY | 134 |

The Silverado drives off down a gently winding road.

MATCH FADE TO:

WINTER has come again, coating the fields in snow.

110.

135   I/E. MARISOL AND TOMMY'S FRONT PORCH/KITCHEN/HALL - DAY   135

CLOSE on a UPS package being placed on the porch. The UPS driver rings the doorbell, leaves without waiting.

INSIDE, Tommy and Marisol deal with breakfast chaos. Time has passed - Luna is now 10, Abbie 8, and their son, MARCO, is nearly 3.

          MARISOL
It's going to be a big weekend.

          TOMMY
    (Playing innocent:)
Why? What's going on this weekend?

          ABBIE
We're having a party.

          LUNA
Someone has a birthday coming up.

          TOMMY
Who?

          MARCO
Me!

          LUNA
Tell him how old you're going to be, Marco.

          MARCO
Three!

As we listen to them talk, PAN along the wall of family photos in the hallway - most of which contain Otto.

In one taken on Halloween, Otto is dressed along with everyone in the family as a *Luchadora*. In the Christmas photo, he's helping the girls assemble a doll house. It seems the family went to a Mexican restaurant for Cinco de Mayo and talked Otto into wearing a sombrero, though he doesn't look happy about it.

Tommy hears the doorbell and goes out onto the front stoop to get the package. He turns to go back inside, then hesitates, staring across the street.

          TOMMY
Marisol?

          MARISOL (O.S.)
What?

                    TOMMY
          Otto hasn't shoveled his walk.

Marisol bursts out of the house and races across the street
ahead of Tommy. She reaches Otto's front door. It is locked.

                    MARISOL
          Get his house keys!

136   INT. OTTO'S FRONT DOOR, HALLWAY - DAY   136

Marisol rushes into the house, keys in hand, her anguish
mounting. Tommy is behind her.

                    MARISOL
          Otto? Otto?

She looks up the stairs.

137   INT. OTTO'S BEDROOM - DAY   137

Marisol enters Otto's bedroom. Otto lies across his side of
the bed at an angle, his feet still on the floor, his shirt
half-buttoned. The Cat is curled up on the bed beside him.

Marisol goes to Otto, touches his face. He is gone. She
weeps.

Tommy appears in the doorway, takes in the scene. He crosses
over to the chair beside Sonia's vanity, grief washing over
him as well. He is about to sit down when he notices the
envelope sticking out from behind the mirror.

Tommy takes the envelope and crosses to Marisol, showing her
that Otto has written "For Marisol" on the envelope.

Marisol takes the envelope, surprised. She opens it and pours
out its contents - a pile of documents, a ring of keys, and
Otto's letter, which she reads.

                    OTTO (V.O.)
          If you're reading this, don't
          worry, I haven't done anything
          stupid. It turns out having a big
          heart isn't as nice as it sounds.
          The doctors warned me it would get
          me in the end, so I planned ahead,
          that's all. I've already had a much
          better run than I expected, thanks
          to Sonya. And you. It turns out you
          were right. You are something.
                    (MORE)

                    OTTO (V.O.) (CONT'D)
          The Cat eats tuna twice a day and
          likes to do his business in private
          - please respect that...

138   INT. CHURCH FUNERAL SERVICE - DAY   138

        A MINISTER speaks at Otto's funeral.

                    OTTO (V.O.)
          I would like a funeral, but nothing
          overblown...

        Marisol and Tommy's family are in the front row, along with
        Malcolm, Jimmy, Andy and Barb, who has brought her dog Prince
        along. Otto's co-workers and Shari Kenzie are there as well.

        Reuben sits in a wheelchair in the aisle; Anita, sitting
        beside him, uses a handkerchief to wipe away his tears.

                    OTTO (V.O.)
          ... Just a remembrance of some sort
          for those people who thought I
          pulled my weight...

138A   EXT. CHURCH RECEPTION HALL - DAY   138A

        Shari Kenzie stands outside the church's reception hall
        discretely reporting as mourners enter the hall behind her.
        Malcolm, who works for Shari now, films the segment.

                    SHARI
          A local hero and good friend of the
          show is being remembered today...

139   INT. CHURCH RECEPTION HALL - DAY   139

        Inside, Mourners gather near a table with food and flowers,
        along with a cake with the same picture of Otto on it that
        Otto's co-workers used for his retirement party cake.

                    OTTO (V.O.)
          My lawyer will give you access to
          my bank accounts.

        Off to one side, Luna shows Abbie a quarter. She grips the
        coin in her fist, blows on the back of her hand, then opens
        her fingers - the coin is gone. Abbie is suitably impressed.

        Marisol and Shari laugh as they tell others about the time
        Otto closed Shari in the garage.

Jimmy wraps Anita and Malcolm in big hugs. Barb sets her plate of cake on the floor, letting her dog Prince eat a portion of Otto's face.

> OTTO (V.O.)
> I never wasted money on crap, so you'll have enough to get the children through school and do what you like with the rest...

A printed sign on the nearby table reads:

> Donations In Otto Anderson's memory may be made to The Sonya Anderson Youth Crisis Fund

140 EXT. CHURCH RECEPTION HALL/PARKING LOT - DAY 140

Marisol, Tommy and the children come out of the reception hall and head for the street.

> OTTO (V.O.)
> The house and everything in it is yours, so long as you promise never to sell it to those real estate bastards...

The family goes to Otto's Chevy, parked in the street. Tommy goes to the driver's side, starts to open the door.

> OTTO (V.O.)
> ... And for God's sake, Marisol, don't let Tommy drive the Chevy.

Marisol appears at Tommy's side, gives him a look. He hands her the car keys, crosses to the passenger side.

> OTTO (V.O.)
> Or anyone else. I'm trusting it with you alone...

The family climbs in the car. Marisol starts the engine.

> OTTO (V.O.)
> ... Because you are NOT an idiot.

As they drive off...

141 EXT. CEMETERY - DAY 141

Otto's name has been carved on the headstone beside Sonya's, the two together again. Pink flowers adorn their graves.

                    OTTO (V.O.)
          Abuelo Otto.
                                                  FADE TO BLACK.
                              THE END

Made in United States
North Haven, CT
30 September 2023